"An intrepid C......... journalist who risked his life to pursue the interviews he records with Mexican officials and victims here, Gibler (*Mexico Unconquered*) recounts an endless litany of violence that has exploded during the tenures of Carlos Salinas, Ernesto Zedillo, Vicente Fox and, especially, Felipe Calderon. . . . Gibler argues passionately to undercut this 'case study in failure.' The drug barons are only getting richer, the murders mount and the police and military repression expand as 'illegality increases the value of the commodity.' With legality, both U.S. and Mexican society could address real issues of substance abuse through education and public-health initiatives. **A visceral, immediate and reasonable argument.**"
—*Kirkus*

"Many writers have pondered the evil and madness of the Mexican/American 'drug war.' Few have analyzed it with such vividness and clarity as John Gibler."
—Howard Campbell, Professor of Anthropology, University of Texas, El Paso

"*To Die in Mexico* shows all the horror of Mexico's current turmoil over drugs—but goes beyond the usual pornography of violence to its critically-informed broader context. Gibler also reveals the brave civic resistance to death cults and official silencing by, among others, some of the remarkable Mexican journalists trying to tell the drug war's hidden story."—Paul Gootenberg, author, *Andean Cocaine: The Making of a Global Drug*

"If you want to cut through the lies, obfuscation and sheer lunacy that surrounds Mexico's so-called drug war, read *To Die in Mexico*. John Gibler reports from Ciudad Juarez, Reynosa, Culiacan—the bloodiest battlegrounds in a fever of violence that has left more than 38,000 dead. But he accepts none of the prevailing myths—that this is a war between rival criminal enterprises, or between a crusading government and assorted barbarous bad guys, that it is a war at all. An antidote to the sensationalism and mythologizing that dominate the discourse, *To Die in Mexico* is at once a gripping read and the smartest, sanest book yet written on the subject in English."—Ben Ehrenreich, author of *The Suitors* and *Ether*

"Gibler is something of a revelation, having been living and writing from Mexico for a range of progressive publications only since 2006, but providing reflections, insights and a level of understanding worthy of a veteran correspondent. His incisive analysis of the causes of injustice in Mexico . . . offers an essential introduction to the country's brutal political and social realities."—Gavin O'Toole, *Latin American Review of Books*

"We are fortunate to have in John Gibler, an astute and thoughtful journalist. Over the past few years, he has reported on conditions and struggles in southern states (Guerrero, Oaxaca, Chiapas) and elsewhere in the country and its northern neighbor. *Mexico Unconquered* shows

us close-ups in the current chapter in a long-running story on our continent. 'Chronicles' isn't precisely apt. Gibler doesn't just serve as a narrator. His prose offers a window into people's lives, letting us meet the participants in revolts, in their days of triumphant success or traumatic repression, in lives of vision, persistence and hope. We spend time beneath the tarps of [the] Oaxaca teachers' *plantón* (protest camp) in the central square. We ride to the hospital alongside a critically-wounded protester in Atenco. We stand in the visitor's line of the prison in Ecatepec. We hear first hand about the ordeals of migration to the US, the violence of the drug war, torture, and disappearances—as well as a daring women's takeover of a [television] station."
—Carwill James, *Left Turn*

"A mix of fast-moving reporting, poetic reflection and wide-ranging historical texts, *Mexico Unconquered* is penned in an accessible and uplifting fashion. A clear historical link is made between the author's close relationships with social movements in both Mexico and in the U.S., making the book a useful tool for those looking to delve deeper into the history and ongoing struggle for revolt and liberation in Mexico."—Stefan Christoff, the *Hour*

"Part journalistic travelogue, part political manifesto, *Mexico Unconquered* recounts some of the more bewildering revolts and upheavals that have roiled Southern Mexico from the turn of the 20th century through contemporary times . . . Gibler is at his best—informative, entertaining, provocative and fluid."—Liliana Valenzuela, the *Texas Observer*

"The pages are quilted passages involving literature reviews, analyses and fierce reporting from talking to 'los de abajo,' or the underdogs, with observations bringing the pueblos alive. His bottom-up chronicle makes him the Howard Zinn (*A People's History of the United States*) for the next generation."—Traci Angel, *Jackson Hole News & Guide*

"Enlightening and informative, *Mexico Unconquered* is a must read."—*Midwest Book Review*

"From Spanish colonization to today's state and corporate repression, *Mexico Unconquered: Chronicles of Power and Revolt*, by John Gibler, is written from the street barricades, against the Slims of the world, and alongside 'the underdogs and rebels' of an unconquered country. The book offers a gripping account of the ongoing attempts to colonize Mexico, and the hopeful grassroots movements that have resisted this conquest."—Benjamin Dangl, *Upside Down World*

"For anyone who has felt confused, confounded, disappointed, disturbed and yet still enchanted by Mexico, John Gibler's *Mexico Unconquered: Chronicles of Power and Revolt* offers some relief. . . . Gibler's interpretation of a 'Mexico unconquered' testifies to the urgency of current struggles, and celebrates the fierce spirit of Mexican resistance, past and present."—*In These Times*

To Die in Mexico

To Die in Mexico

Dispatches from Inside the Drug War

John Gibler

Open Media Series | City Lights Books

The Open Media Series is edited by Greg Ruggiero and archived by
the Tamiment Library, New York University.

Library of Congress Cataloging-in-Publication Data
Gibler, John.
To die in Mexico: dispatches from inside the drug war / John Gibler.
    p. cm. — (Open media series)
 ISBN 978-0-87286-517-4
1. Drug traffic—Mexico. 2. Drug control—Mexico. 3. Drug traffic—
United States. 4. Drug control—United States. I. Title. II. Series.

HV5840.M4G53 2011
363.450972—dc22

                    2011002970

City Lights Books are published at the City Lights Bookstore
261 Columbus Avenue, San Francisco, CA 94133

Visit our website: www.citylights.com

CONTENTS

Morir en México, (To Die in Mexico), by Antonio Helguera. Published in Mexico by *La Jornada* on March 15, 2010. The gravestones read clockwise from the left: "She must have been into something; It was a gang feud; They murdered amongst themselves; What was he doing at that hour?; It was a settling of accounts; She dressed provocatively; Who knows what he was getting into; She was a whore."

ONE

Silence demands that its enemies disappear suddenly and without a trace.
—Ryszard Kapuscinski

THE BARE FACTS ARE SO TERRIFYING they pass beyond the edge of anything credible. Who would believe, for example, that the warden of a state prison would let convicted killers out at night and loan them official vehicles, automatic assault rifles, and bulletproof vests, so that they could gun down scores of innocent people in a neighboring state and then quickly hop back over the state line and into prison, behind bars, a perfect alibi? Who would believe that a paramilitary drug-trafficking organization formed by ex–Special Forces of the Mexican Army would kidnap a local cop and torture him into confessing all of the above details about the prisoners' death squad, videotape the confession, execute the cop on camera with a shot to the heart, and then post the video on YouTube? Who could fathom that the federal attorney general would, within hours of the video-taped confession and execution being posted online, arrest the warden, and then a few days later hold a press conference fully acknowledging that the prisoners' death squad had operated for months, killing ten people in a bar in January 2010, eight people in a bar in May 2010, and seventeen people at a birthday party in July?

Difficult to believe, but all of it is true.

The city is Torreón, in Coahuila state, which shares a border with Texas. On January 31, 2010, an armed convoy attacked three bars in Torreón, killing ten people and wounding forty. Five months later, on May 15, an armed convoy attacked the inauguration party of a new bar in Torreón, killing eight people and wounding twenty. On July 18, at about 1:30 a.m., an armed convoy pulled up to a private birthday party at the Quinta Italia Inn in Torreón. Five men wearing bulletproof vests and carrying AR-15 assault rifles crashed into the party hall, shooting indiscriminately. They killed seventeen people, including Carlos Antonio Mota Méndez, who was celebrating his thirty-first birthday, his brother, Héctor José, and four members of the hired band, Ríos. They wounded another eighteen people. After each massacre the killers drove back across the Durango-Coahuila state line to the Centro de Readaptación Social de Gómez Palacio, the Gómez Palacio prison, or "Social Re-adaptation Center." Prison director Margarita Rojas Rodríguez had left instructions for the prisoners to be allowed back inside without a fuss.

But no one would have believed this. The drug war body count rose, headlines tabulated the dead at each massacre scene, and federal investigators speculated that the bar owners must have had some links to organized crime. The dead, somehow, must have been dirty. And then on Thursday, July 23, 2010, someone posted a video online that was quickly reposted on a website called *blogdelnarco.com*.

You may want to look away.

The video begins with three men in the frame—the image is a little shaky, the resolution low. Two men stand with AR-15 assault rifles, wearing T-shirts, military vests loaded with clips, and what look like stylized solid-black hockey masks that cover their faces from beneath the chin to above the forehead. The third man, between them, is on his knees, shirtless, hands tied behind his back. Only his face and part of his torso are visible in the frame. A voice off camera asks, "What is your name?" The kneeling man responds, "Rodolfo Nájera."

Nájera's face is deformed. The swelling under his left eye makes it look as if a rock had been surgically implanted under his skin. His left ear is only half attached. Blood streams from this ear and down his chest. Nájera looks at the camera and answers quickly and precisely all questions. He knows the men with the camera will kill him.

"What do you do?" the voice from off camera asks.

"I am a Lerdo police officer," Nájera responds.

He speaks with difficulty. His voice seems unnaturally low, in contrast to the voice off camera that enunciates clearly, forcefully, and calmly, with the articulation of one accustomed to exercising authority.

"Age?"

"Thirty-five."

"Whom do you work for?"

Nájera pauses for a beat. "For the Pirate."

"Who are those?"

"Some Lerdo pushers." Nájera uses the term *puchadores*, which comes from the English term pusher and refers to street dealers.

The video has been edited; it cuts in and out. The trails of blood that run down Nájera's chest multiply and elongate each time the image jumps forward in time. The off-camera voice asks who controls the runners. The Pirate. He asks whom the Pirate works for. Nájera says the Delta.

"Who is the Delta?"

"A guy in the prison."

Nájera is developing a twitch, his head jerks to the right and back.

"What is the Delta's name?"

"Daniel Gabriel."

"And this guy, what's his deal? What's his job? What does he do?"

"He sends the killers out to murder people."

"What's he doing at the prison?"

"He got busted with drugs and guns."

"He's a prisoner?"

"Yes."

"How often does he leave the prison?"

"Everyday after eight at night."

"Who lets him leave?"

"The warden."

"What is the warden's name?"

"I don't know her name."

There is a pause and you can hear voices in the background. You can hear other voices that sound as if they are coming through radios, police radios. You can hear the wind blowing into the camera's microphone and see the wind shaking the tree branches in the background. The man to Nájera's left in a blue T-shirt looks down to the ground and shifts his weight from one foot to the other and back again, then looks into the camera. He is wearing a baseball cap turned backward under his mask. He is several inches shorter than the man on the right, and seems thin, pale, and very young.

The off-camera voice asks for names, nicknames, and ranks of the police and government officials that provide protection to the prison death squad. Nájera struggles, but provides a name each time the voice asks, "And who else?" At this point the camera zooms in on Nájera's face. His right eye is swollen shut. There are bruises, cuts, and burn marks across his face. Nájera provides another name and is met instantly with the same question, "And who else?" He pauses, twitches. The man in the blue T-shirt to his left looks from the camera down at him, then calmly reaches out to his semi-detached ear and folds it down. Nájera provides another name. And then another, and another, and another until the camera cuts.

In the next frame Nájera is out of breath, struggling.

The man in the blue T-shirt is standing slightly behind him, pointing his rifle at his back. The voice asks who is this Güero Pollero. (The nickname means roughly "Blond Smuggler.") Nájera says that he is the one who goes out with the death squads to kill people in bars in Torreón. The voice asks who sent him and why. Nájera says that a man named Arturo, who is rumored to have fled to Guadalajara, sent the Güero Pollero to bring heat down on the Zetas in Torreón. Here you can hear another voice off camera to Nájera's left, coaching him. The men with the guns are Zetas, members of the ex-Special Forces cartel that has been the main target of federal anti-narcotics operations throughout President Felipe Calderón's drug war. In a brief pause while Nájera answers the why question, the voice off camera to the left nudges him on, saying, "To bring heat down on us." Nájera follows the cue quickly, speaking over the off-camera voice, "To bring heat down on the Zetas."

The voice leading the interrogation asks, "Who killed the people at the Quinta Italia?"

Nájera, "The same, Güero Pollero and his people, following Arturo's orders."

Nájera goes on to describe how the killers leave the prison heavily armed, wearing bulletproof vests, driving prison vehicles. You can hear an off-camera voice whisper advice to whoever is leading the interview. Nájera describes how the prison warden allows the killers to leave prison grounds, knowing full well that they are going out to murder. He repeats the details several times: the men leaving the prison at night in prison vehicles, with prison weapons, to kill innocent people in the territory of the Zetas, and the warden allowing it all to take place.

The video is nine minutes and fifty-four seconds long. At 9:21, the frame cuts and it is suddenly night. The men with guns are on opposite sides of Nájera. A loud mechanical noise fills the microphone, a generator perhaps, or a truck engine. Headlights and flashlights illuminate Nájera's beaten face. The blood running down his chest is now one thick current. A voice off camera says that those of "the last letter" don't commit acts of barbarism or kill innocent people. The voice asks why then the Gómez Palacio gang would kill the innocent in their territory. The voice asks if they prefer to kill innocent people because they can't face "the last letter," the Zetas, or Z's. Nájera responds, "Yes sir."

"Because they can't defeat us?"

"No sir."

The frame cuts again. Nájera kneels alone now. Two shadows step away, one to each side. A shot rings out and he pitches forward.

The video was posted on a Thursday night. The next morning federal officers detained Margarita Rojas Rodríguez, the warden of the prison in Gómez Palacio, and three other prison officials. On Sunday, the spokesperson for the federal attorney general's office announced the arrests and the death squad's responsibility for the recent massacres in Torreón but did not mention the video posted on *blogdelnarco.com*.

A DEATH WITH NO NAME. A death that extinguishes who you were along with who you are. A death that holds you before the world as a testament only to death itself. All that is left is your body destroyed in a vacant lot, hanging from a highway overpass, or locked in the trunk of a car. Your name is severed, cut off, and discarded. The only history that remains attached to your body is that of your particular death: bullet holes, burns, slashes, contusions, limbs removed. The executioners of this killing ground destroy each person twice. First they obliterate your world; if you are lucky, they do so with a spray of bullets. But then, once you are gone, they will turn your body from that of a person into that of a message. You will appear as a flash on a television screen. You will be printed on tabloid front pages in full color and strung up on the sides of newspaper stands in cities across the country, your disfigured body hanging next to soccer players and bikini-clad models. You will lose your name. You will lose your past, the record of your loves and fears, triumphs and failures, and all the small things in between. Those who look upon you will see only death.

But names travel too far to be entirely erased or destroyed. Names always leave a trace. Even when they kill you, dismantle your body, or bind it in duct tape, and leave your remains on the side of the road, your name waits.

José Humberto Márquez Compeán. He was found like so many: tortured, killed, wrapped in a blanket (*encobijado* is the term of art), and discarded in a vacant lot on the edge of San Nicolás de los Garza, near Monterrey in Nuevo León,

Mexico. At first glance he would appear to be only another death to add to the body count of 22,000 drugland executions in Mexico between December 2006, when President Felipe Calderón of the rightwing National Action Party (PAN) launched his self-proclaimed "war" against drug traffickers, and late March 2010, when a local reporter photographed Márquez Compeán's body lying lifeless and bound across a dry scratch of earth. Such were the facts: death, a beaten corpse, a barren field in San Nicolás de los Garza. Behind these facts one can glimpse the intentions of those who killed Compeán and dumped his body there: to end his life and turn his body into a nameless mass of death.

But there was a glitch. The reporter assigned to the story saw beyond the message of death. By sheer coincidence Francisco Cantú, a 37-year-old reporter for *Multimedios* in Monterrey, recognized a coffee-colored shirt with an orange letter B stitched over the chest. Cantú had seen the shirt and the man wearing it, José Humberto Márquez Compeán, only hours before. In fact, he had photographed Compeán only hours before.

Cantú had just started his shift at 5:30 a.m. that Monday morning when his editor told him there was a shoot-out in San Nicolás de los Garza. Cantú hit the road, but then got a call while he was en route. There was no gun battle, but rather a body found in an abandoned lot, his editor said. He might as well take the picture anyway. Cantú kept driving and was the first reporter on the scene. "I took the first photos from a distance," Cantú told me, "and then I slowly got closer to see if the authorities would say anything." When he noticed that the police were not paying attention, he walked right up to the body to take more photographs. "I take the photo and when I look at it and I see the B on the shirt I say, Oh damn! This is the same guy from yesterday."

To confirm his observation, he went back to his car and opened his laptop to review and compare images from the day before. "I can see that it is the same person," Cantú said, "because of the T-shirt, he had that same brown shirt, but his face was all beaten. His face was messed up." The man lying dead on Monday morning in San Nicolás de los Garza was the same person, José Humberto Márquez Compeán, that Cantú had photographed on Sunday afternoon in perfectly good health. In the first set of images, Compeán is walking with his hands tied behind him, looking down, an expression that appears caught between stoicism and dread on his face. Soldiers from the Mexican navy surround him, and then lead him into the back of a navy pickup truck. Compeán is in military custody, handcuffed, uninjured, surrounded by heavily armed soldiers. It is Sunday afternoon. He would next appear before the world on Monday morning as a dead body in a field.

Compeán's wife, Hilda Rodríguez, told Cantú and his colleagues at Milenio Televisión, a branch of Multimedios, "I saw him in the news, how they put him in a police truck and then a helicopter, and then he turns up dead. Why did they kill him? Who killed him? I want justice. I have three children."

On Sunday, March 21, 2010, a convoy of municipal police in Santa Catarina, Nuevo León, detained Compeán and José Adrián Lucio Barajas. The convoy was on its way to the municipal hall when the police supposedly spotted the two men selling drugs. Santa Catarina security chief René Castillo and police chief Luis Eduardo Murrieta were on board and in command of the police convoy. They stopped, detained the two men at gunpoint, roughing up Barajas in the process. Minutes later an unidentified convoy of presumed drug assassins attacked the police, killing two guards and a bystander and wounding the police chief. The police retreated to the station to wait for a navy escort to take the wounded to a hospital.

When Cantú arrived at the scene of the shoot-out at around 2:00 p.m. on Sunday, he heard that an official had been wounded and taken back to the police station. After taking photographs of the scene, he went to the station. When he arrived the navy and police had cordoned off the area. The police tried to stop him from taking photographs, but he was able to slip past the cordon and keep working. The navy started to escort the wounded out of the station. "First they took out the wounded guy [Barajas] and then they took out the wounded official, but with a hood over his head," Cantú said. "Then they took out this other person who was wearing a coffee-colored T-shirt with an orange letter B on it. That struck me, those colors, and so I took his photo." Cantú captured the images of soldiers leading the wounded and detained first to navy trucks and then later onto a navy helicopter. He mentioned the man in a brown shirt in the story he filed that evening. After that, no one seems to know what happened to Compeán, how exactly he went from being held handcuffed in navy custody to, some fourteen hours later, lying wrapped in a blanket, dead, in San Nicolás de los Garza.

On Monday morning, upon discovering that he had photographed Compeán in navy custody only hours before photographing him dead, Cantú called his editors and sent the pair of images. The Mexican national media picked up the story within hours. Navy officials said in a press release that they only lent their support to municipal authorities by taking the police chief, Barajas, and Compeán to a nearby hospital. After that, the press release said, they turned everyone over to municipal authorities and do not know what happened. Witnesses at the hospital told the Nuevo León correspondent for *La Jornada*, Mexico's largest left-leaning daily newspaper, that they saw the chief, Murrieta, get off the helicopter and enter the hospital for treatment, but they never saw Compeán get off the helicopter. The Santa Catarina municipal officials said that federal authorities maintained custody of Compeán, not them. "I don't know. I don't know. I don't know. That's my position," René Castillo, the chief of security who, together with Murrieta, originally detained Compeán and Barajas, told the Associated Press at the time. Murrieta and Castillo both disappeared for a few weeks, and then quietly returned to their posts. No one has been charged with the murder of José Humberto Márquez

Compeán. The barren lot where Cantú photographed Compeán's dead body is only about a three-minute drive from the regional naval base.

Hilda Rodríguez's questions—"Why did they kill him? Who killed him?"—are those that the practice of anonymous death, the killing and ritual depositing of the mutilated person's body, tries to render impossible to answer. If a body is just a body, who will step forward to ask why someone was killed and who killed him or her? If a body has no name or history, then who will demand justice? When a person's ruined body is crafted into a message, the meaning is clear: This can happen to *you*. The dead must have done something to end up like that—crossed a line, spoken up—so better to do nothing, better to look away.

Anonymous death needs silence. Names are thus dissolved. Facts vanquished. Times and locations obscured. Who was she? No one says a thing. Why did they kill him? Not a word. How is it possible that they could massacre all those people and simply drive away? No one poses the question. But if he was last seen in navy custody? Do not ask. Who controls this town? Where does she live? What businesses does he own? All questions you can get killed for asking. Silence is essential. Where murder is part of the overhead in an illicit multibillion-dollar industry, impunity becomes a fundamental investment. And impunity cannot hold without silence. Hence Mexico has become the most dangerous country in the hemisphere for journalists, those whose labor requires voice. Mexico's "drug war" has become one of the most perilous beats in the world. Sixty-eight reporters have been gunned down since 2000—forty-seven of them slain between July 2008 and September 2010—and at least fifteen disappeared since 2006; which is to say, silenced. How many of those murder cases have been solved? Not one. How many of the disappeared journalists have been located? Not one. Silence travels in armed convoys of twenty to fifty highly trained assassins equipped with military-issue assault rifles and fragmentation grenades. Those who labor in the terrain of voice carry notebooks and pens, cameras, and tripods.

At 7:00 a.m. on April 6, 2007, Amado Ramírez Dillanes, a 50-year-old reporter with both Televisa and Radiorama in Acapulco, Guerrero, finished his daily one-hour radio program without a glitch. He left the Radiorama studio at around 7:20 a.m. and walked to his parked car on La Paz Street in the bustling center of Acapulco, a block from the town square, a few yards from a police station, and right in front of the California Hotel. As Ramírez Dillanes opened the driver's door, a gunman approached him from behind and opened fire with a .38-caliber pistol, hitting him twice. Ramírez Dillanes ran to seek refuge or help in the California Hotel. The gunman followed and shot Ramírez Dillanes in the back. The gunman then walked away. Five minutes later Ramírez Dillanes was dead. Scores of tourists and local residents witnessed the murder. More than one hundred police officers, detectives, and forensics experts from six different municipal and federal agencies arrived on the scene an hour later. No one has been charged with the murder of Ramírez Dillanes.

On the night of September 23, 2008, Alejandro Xenón Fonseca Estrada, a well-known journalist with the radio station EXA FM in Villahermosa, Tabasco, set out to hang banners across town denouncing a surge in kidnappings in Tabasco and across Mexico. One banner read simply: NO TO KIDNAPPING!!! Fonseca Estrada was standing up on top of a truck parked on the corner of Paseo Tabasco and Adolfo Ruiz Cortines hanging up a banner when a group of men in an SUV pulled up and asked him what he was doing. Hanging this banner, he said. They told him to take it down. He refused. They ordered him to climb down and get in the car. He refused. One man grabbed an AR-15 assault rifle, held it out the car window, and fired into Fonseca Estrada's chest. He died. They drove away.

On the evening of May 25, 2009, Eliseo Barrón Hernández was at home in the town of Gómez Palacio, Durango, with his wife and two daughters. Barrón Hernández worked for ten years as a reporter for the newspaper *La Opinión* in the neighboring city of Torreón, Coahuila. He had recently published articles about a police corruption scandal in Torreón that led to the firing of some three hundred police officers. On May 25, eleven masked gunmen broke in, beat him in front of his family, and took him away. Twenty-six hours later his dead body was found in a ditch with five bullet wounds and signs of having been tortured. During his funeral the next day five banners signed by Joaquín "El Chapo" Guzmán were hung across Torreón warning journalists to be more careful. One of the banners read: WE ARE HERE, JOURNALISTS. ASK ELISEO BARRÓN. EL CHAPO AND THE CARTEL DO NOT FORGIVE. BE CAREFUL, SOLDIERS AND JOURNALISTS. A few weeks later the Mexican army produced a few suspects detained in unrelated events who had supposedly confessed to murdering Barrón Hernández on orders from the Zetas, the enemies of El Chapo. In April 2010, a spokeswoman for the attorney general told representatives from the Committee to Protect Journalists that she could say nothing about the suspects' whereabouts or trial date. On May 31, 2010, Barrón Hernández's friend and colleague Julián Parra Ibarra published an editorial on the passing of one year since Barrón Hernández's murder. The investigation had gone nowhere, with no further arrests, no trial, and no information about the supposedly confessed killers. Parra Ibarra concluded, "Nothing has changed, and worse still, no one says anything."

Silence.

Valentín Valdés Espinosa was a 29-year-old local news reporter and the cofounder of the newspaper *Zócalo de Saltillo* in Coahuila. On January 7, 2010, he and two colleagues left work around 10:45 p.m. A few minutes later two SUVs cut them off. Gunmen forced Valdés Espinosa and one of his colleagues into the vehicles and drove away. The colleague, whose name was not released, was set free sometime later. Valdés Espinosa's body, bearing bullet wounds and signs of torture, was found a few hours later in front of a motel. A handwritten poster board sign was left over his chest: THIS IS GOING TO HAPPEN TO THOSE WHO DON'T UNDERSTAND. THE MESSAGE IS FOR EVERYONE.

And yet people talk, or sometimes whisper. The drive to understand, the drive to communicate is unstoppable, though it may be forced into hiding, sent scurrying into the myriad corners of private life. Most everywhere one travels in Mexico one can hear people talking, lamenting, debating, and marveling over the latest headlines from the drug war. Silence does not often seek as its prey the murmurs of rumor and small talk. Silence—this special breed of paramilitarized narco-silence—takes aim at a particular type of speaking that has, typically, two characteristics: it may be heard by many and it enunciates facts that are bad for business.

For drug war silence is not the mere absence of talking, but rather the practice of not saying anything. You may talk as much as you like, as long as you avoid facts. Newspaper headlines announce the daily death toll, but the articles will not tell you anything about who the dead were, who might have killed them, or why. No detailed descriptions based on witness testimony. No investigation. The same goes for the homicide detectives tasked with investigating the murder. They will arrive on the scene, count the bullet casings, snap a few photographs of the body, and file it all away. Politicians might denounce violence in the abstract, but they refrain from ever mentioning the names of those fighting over the territory in their districts.

And yet people across Mexico still challenge this reign of silence, this bullet-imposed public ban on facts. As a result they often find themselves looking down the barrel of a gun into the eyes of silence. Journalists, human rights activists, family members of murder victims, rural guerrilla fighters, and occasionally, honest government officials are those most often within the crosshairs of silence. Their speaking is a combat tactic in the battle against anonymous death; theirs is a true battle, not against plants and those who like to use them to get high, but against the insidious regime of illegality and impunity that makes the drug business such good money, and that imposes the death and silence necessary to keep it that way. These are people who still, despite all the blood and broken promises, believe in some form of justice—if not the justice of the state, of the law, of police and courts and legislators, then the justice of knowing, for speaking and contributing to knowledge are forms of rebellion against silence and murder. The bloated profits to be had in the illegal narcotics market require that vast and complex networks of human activity—farming, processing, packaging, international shipping, warehousing, distribution and sales, arms trafficking, surveillance, money laundering, and extensive political protection—remain submerged in a nebulous space of constant talking and perpetually enforced ignorance.

The stories and voices of those who rebel against silence and anonymous death are the heart of this book.

THIS IS WHAT THEY DO NOT WANT YOU TO SAY: The Mexican army and federal police have administered drug trafficking for decades. Drug money fills the vaults of Mexico's banks, enters the national economy at every level, and, with traffickers' annual profits estimated at between $30 billion and $60 billion a year, rivals oil as the largest single source of cash revenue in the country. (And Mexico is not the only place where this is so.) The chief national *capos*, or drug lords, are not only the most wanted narcos of the day—such as Joaquín "El Chapo" Guzmán—but also generals in the Mexican army and commanders of the federal police. The federal police forces are the main recruitment center for mid-level drug-trafficking operators. The army and the state police are the main recruitment centers for the enforcers, the paramilitary units in charge of assassinations, and the armed protection of drugs and mid- and high-level operators. According to the federal government's own estimate, people working for the various illegal narcotics businesses have directly infiltrated more than half of the municipal police forces in the country. During the seventy-one-year reign of the Institutional Revolutionary Party (PRI), the Mexican army controlled the division of territory for drug production and trafficking routes, allocating sub-divisions to local franchises, colloquially called cartels. A given territory under a cartel's control is known as a *plaza*. Murder has always been a part of settling business deals gone wrong and of fighting for control of a *plaza*. People who fall in police busts and stand guilty before the television cameras are either those who have fallen out of favor and are thus turned over to the cops, or those who have been betrayed—by federal officials interested in selling the *plaza* to someone new or by former allies interested in taking it over. Producing arrests is a necessary feature of the industry, and so, like murder, arrest becomes a way of settling accounts or invading territory. High-level federal officials in United States government know all of this and go along with the theatrics, because, among other reasons, the U.S. economy is also buoyed by the influx of drug money. The defense industries profit handsomely from arms sales to armies, police, and the drug gangs themselves; the police are addicted to asset forfeiture laws; prison guard unions are addicted to budget increases; and the criminalization of drugs has proven a durable excuse to lock people of color in prison in a country still shackled by racism.

The so-called "drug war" in Mexico is really two wars, a war between disciplined, organized, and intensely well-funded trafficking organizations in which the state also participates, and a media spectacle that presents combat and arrests as the product of diligent law-enforcement operations. The current, overlapping drug wars in Mexico date to the so-called democratic transition period between 1994 and 2006. During the six-year term of Carlos Salinas (1988–1994), the Gulf Cartel bloomed from a loosely organized group of runners into one of the most powerful transnational criminal enterprises in the hemisphere, and one capable of competing with the longer-standing Sinaloan cartels based in Tijuana, Guadalajara, Culiacán, and Ciudad Juárez. Salinas's successor, Ernesto Zedillo, furious with Salinas for leaving him with the 1994 peso crisis that battered the Mexican economy, attacked the Gulf Cartel. His administration arrested and extradited to the United States the Gulf capo Juan García Ábrego. Zedillo also imprisoned Salinas's own brother, Raúl, for "illicit enrichment" (Swiss banks froze almost $100 million in accounts that Raúl had opened under false names) and involvement in the murder of José Francisco Ruiz Massieu. Then chair of the PRI and set to become the PRI majority leader in the Mexican Chamber of Deputies, Ruiz Massieu was also Raúl and Carlos Salinas's ex-brother-in-law. When the PRI lost the 2000 presidential elections and Vicente Fox and the PAN took control of the presidency, Fox and the PAN also favored the Sinaloa Cartel over the Gulf Cartel. El Chapo—the presumed head of the Sinaloa Cartel—escaped from a maximum-security prison in a laundry basket six weeks after Fox's inauguration. The Fox administration orchestrated the capture and extradition to the United States of García Ábrego's successor, Osiel Cárdenas Guillén, the capo and mastermind who created the paramilitary Zetas unit in 1997 by recruiting from within the Mexican army's Special Forces units created by Zedillo as counterinsurgency shock troops, and then sent to kill Cárdenas. But by 2004 the Sinaloan trafficking organizations loosely allied as The Federation began to fracture, and former allies turned upon each other, vying for territorial supremacy and thus initiating a drugland civil war

that began to rage throughout the country. By the end of
Fox's six-year term in 2006, the war was full on, and literally,
heads were rolling. Calderón entered office in December
2006, after widespread accusations of electoral fraud that
led to months of huge protests. Calderón refused to agree
to a full recount of the votes and had to sneak into Congress
at midnight for his inauguration in order to avoid protester
blockades. The electoral protests were not isolated. Mexico
in 2006 was gripped with powerful social mobilizations such
as the Zapatistas' Other Campaign and the teachers' rebellion in Oaxaca. Calderón staked his presidency on sending
the army into the streets to wage "war" on drug traffickers
and send an unequivocal message of military might to the
massive protest movements that had surged throughout the
country in the preceding months.

Calderón's "war," however, has mostly targeted the Gulf
Cartel, the Zetas, the Carrillo Fuentes, or Juárez Cartel,
the Beltrán Leyva Cartel, and the Familia Michoacana, and
has left the Sinaloa Cartel more or less alone. A National
Public Radio analysis of 2,600 drug-related federal arrests
between December 2006 and May 2010 found that members of the Sinaloa Cartel accounted for only 12 percent of
arrestees. According to Mexican federal government statistics the Sinaloa Cartel is responsible for 84 percent of the
recent drug-war murders. In November 2008 federal police
arrested Noé Ramírez Mandujano, the director of Mexico's
national counter-narcotics agency, for accepting a bribe of
$450,000 from the Beltrán Leyvas' Pacific Cartel, then the

archenemy of the Sinaloa Cartel. In December 2009, navy commandos stormed the high-end Cuernavaca apartment complex where Arturo Beltrán Leyva, leader of the Pacific Cartel, was hiding out. The soldiers killed him, stripped his body naked, and carefully laid out his money and jewelry over the bullet-ridden corpse.

His war has also created a climate of such overwhelming violence and impunity that assassinations of political opponents—indigenous rights leaders, human rights advocates, anti-mining activists, guerrilla insurgents—are quickly swept into the ever rising body count without much attention or outcry. Paramilitaries shot and killed Beatriz Cariño and Jyri Jaakkola in broad daylight as they participated in a human rights caravan taking food and medical supplies to the besieged Triqui indigenous community of San Juan Copala in the state of Oaxaca. No one has been arrested; the federal government did not send police to break the paramilitary barricade on the highway leading to Copala. Raúl Lucas Lucía and Manuel Ponce Ríos, two indigenous rights activists in Guerrero state were tortured an executed in February 2010. No arrests were made. Activists have been murdered in Chiapas, Sinaloa, Baja California, and Chihuahua states; all the cases remain unsolved.

In the United States, both George W. Bush and Barack Obama have sent money, arms, and military aid to Mexico's army and federal police to help them "combat" drug trafficking. U.S. officials and most of the major U.S. press outlets forget the long list of federal police and generals who later became known as top-level narcos—Rafael Aguilar Guajardo, Miguel Angel Félix Gallardo, Amado Carillo Fuentes, Osiel Cárdenas, Guillermo González Calderoni, Jesús Gutiérrez Rebollo—when approving or covering U.S. aid to the Mexican federal government, such as the $1.4 billion Mérida Initiative. U.S. officials and the press routinely neglect to mention that the Mexican army and federal police very often *are* drug traffickers.

Drugs are big business. The United Nations 2010 World Drug Report estimates that the global cocaine and opiates markets generate $153 billion a year. The U.N. estimates the global drug industry to generate between $300 and $500 billion. Cannabis is the most widely consumed illegal drug, but it is more difficult to estimate its annual revenues since it can be grown and sold locally worldwide in small amounts. The quasi-legal marijuana crop in the State of California alone was worth an estimated $17 billion in 2008; the value of all of California's legal field crops in 2008 was $4.19 billion. The 2010 U.S. Department of State's International Narcotics Control Strategy Report estimates that Mexican drug-trafficking organizations move up to $25 billion in earnings across the U.S. border into Mexico every year. The Mexican federal government estimates that drug traffickers earned over $132 billion between December 2006 and June 2010. Mexico's "most wanted" *capo*—El Chapo Guzmán—is now a recurring figure on the *Forbes* list of billionaires. The first year Guzmán appeared on the list, 2009, the magazine editors listed the source of his fortune, as "shipping."

Estimates are suspect. The government numbers for how many billions of dollars are earned in the business, how many tons of product are successfully moved across borders, how many people get high on a regular basis, and how many people only briefly experiment with illegal drugs are mostly guesses, some perhaps intelligent, some driven by ulterior motives, and some just wild. The United Nations 1994 estimate that the global illegal drug market was worth some $500 billion a year is really just conjecture. No one knows. Drug barons do not submit (accurate) income tax returns. But these numbers, whether they are a bit high or a bit low, do indicate the sheer scale of both the marketplace for illegal narcotics and the failure of interdiction efforts.

Drugs are commodities. People have been consuming cannabis and coca for at least two thousand years. Poppies were first domesticated some eight thousand years ago, and in 1552 BCE Theban physicians had more than 700 medicinal recipes for the use of opiates. Successive United States governments have spearheaded and imposed a global prohibition regime banning the consumption of these and other plants and chemicals for the past hundred years. Along with coffee, tea, tobacco, and sugar, these plants were essential commodities in the formation of Western European capitalism over the past five hundred years. The fact that they are now illegal is what makes the business of shipping and selling them so amazingly profitable. Illegality is now a part of their commodity form. A Colombian farmer will take in no more than $1,000 for the 100 kilograms of coca leaves used to make a kilogram of basic coca paste. Three kilos of paste will make one kilo of processed cocaine. Once that kilo of cocaine hits the streets in the United States of America, it will be worth $100,000, or about $100 a gram. In the Colombian country-side the exact same substance is worth no more than $3,000. Arriving in Mexico, it is worth about $12,500. By the time it reaches Seattle or Columbus or Baltimore, its value will increase by over 3,000 percent. Growing the plant used to make cocaine is not good money. Moving cocaine into the United States is insanely good money.

The business of transporting cocaine, marijuana, hero-in, and methamphetamines is so profitable precisely because those drugs are illegal. Legalization would slash the mas-sive profit margin that illegality creates. As California voters faced a ballot initiative to legalize marijuana in the sum-mer of 2010, the right-wing RAND Drug Policy Research Center released estimates that marijuana prices would fall by 90 percent upon legalization and regulation: a $375 ounce of medical marijuana could be worth $38 an ounce upon statewide legalization. But medical marijuana is grown in California and already quasi-legal (legal under state law and illegal under federal law). The price for illegal drugs from Mexico and South America might plummet even further. Legalization would put the traffickers as they exist today out of business.

Illegality creates complications as well as spectacular profits. First, one has to do something with the mass of cash, the sheer bulk of paper money. Drug lords need banks.

A glimpse: *Bloomberg Markets* magazine's August 2010 issue reported that drug traffickers who used a DC-9 jet to move cocaine from South America to Mexico had purchased the jet "with laundered funds they transferred through two of the biggest banks in the U.S.: Wachovia Corp. and Bank of America Corp." The Mexican newsweekly *Proceso* reported that the Mexican banking industry finds itself with an "extra" $10 billion in cash every year. The Mexican Treasury Secretary said in a press conference on June 15, 2010, that the forty-one banks operating in Mexico have "ten billion dollars that cannot be explained within the proper dynamics of the country's economic activity."

But banks also need drug lords. In 2008, drug money saved the major global banks from collapse and thus, stretching just a bit, saved capitalism from a devastating internal crisis when the speculative capital markets imploded. Drug money—truckloads of cash, actual physical money—would appear to be one of capitalism's global savings accounts. In December 2009, Rajeev Syal at *The Observer* in London reported, "Drugs money worth billions of dollars kept the financial system afloat at the height of the global crisis." Antonio Maria Costa, the head of the UN Office on Drugs and Crime, told Syal that he had seen "evidence that the proceeds of organized crime were 'the only liquid investment capital' available to some banks on the brink of collapse [in 2008]. He said that a majority of the $352bn (£216bn) of drugs profits was absorbed into the economic system as a result."

Christian De Brie wrote in *Le Monde Diplomatique* in April 2000 that over $350 billion of illicit cash is successfully laundered and reinvested globally *every year*, nearly $1 billion a day. Here is his math, "The annual profits from drug trafficking (cannabis, cocaine, heroin) are estimated at $300–500bn (not to mention the rapidly mushrooming synthetic drugs), that is 8% to 10% of world trade. Computer piracy has a turnover in excess of $200bn, counterfeit goods $100bn, European Community budget fraud $10-15bn, animal smuggling $20bn, etc. In all, and counting only activities with a transnational dimension, including the white slave trade, the world's gross criminal product totals far above $1,000bn a year, nearly 20% of world trade." He writes that if half of that goes to overhead, that leaves $500 billion in profit. If one-third of that amount goes to the laundry services of banks and investors, that would leave $350 billion in profit fully integrated into the "legal" capitalist economy every year.

Black market entrepreneurs also like to diversify their investment portfolios. Besides laundering their cash through myriad businesses in the legal economy, today's transnational drug barons are expanding, for example, into oil. A report in the *Washington Post* in December 2009 details how the Zetas and other cartels stole more than $1 billion of oil from the Mexican national oil company Pemex between 2008 and the end of 2009. In the cases described in the *Washington Post*, the Zetas tapped directly into federal pipelines and siphoned the oil off to stolen tanker trucks, which they then used to sell the fuel to a range of Texas-based oil companies like Y Gas and Oil and Trammo Petroleum. Pemex officials said they detected $715 million of stolen oil in 2008 alone. And apparently the Zetas are not the only ones working the stolen oil market: company officials found 396 illegal taps throughout all of Mexico's thirty-one states. In 2010, oil theft increased by another 75 percent. In December 2010, an oil pipeline in Puebla state exploded, killing twenty-eight people, including thirteen children. Pemex director Juan José Suárez Coppel blamed the blast on an illegal tap.

Those in the illicit drug business add to their profits with income from human trafficking, kidnapping, extortion, and even cattle rustling. Edmundo Ramírez Martínez authored a report for the Mexican legislature on the perils Central American migrants face while crossing Mexico en route to the United States. He estimated that the drug organizations' control over human trafficking along the border brings them another $3 billion a year. Another report from the Mexican legislature states that kidnapping has increased 300 percent in the past five years. The report calculates that drug gangs participated in 30 percent of the recent kidnappings while soldiers and police made up 22 percent of the nation's kidnappers. On one balmy day in August 2010 in Tamaulipas state, gunmen executed seventy-two Central and South American migrants in a barn. Soon after, the National Human Rights Commission reported having received 198 witness accounts of kidnappings involving nearly ten thousand migrants, all in the first six months of 2009. In Ciudad

Juárez, extortion and kidnapping have driven thousands of small and medium-sized businesses to ruin, prompting the closure of ten thousand businesses in the past three years. Under the headline "Crime steals cattle and sells on the formal market," the daily newspaper *El Universal* wrote in September 2010 that at least eleven states show an increase of 30 to 50 percent in cattle rustling. Ranchers "attribute the increase to the growth of organized crime and the fact that the drug-trafficking cartels are expanding their field of activities."

And then there are the guns. In Mexico, federal law prohibits open gun sales and the permits granted directly from the Secretary of Defense are extremely rare. In the U.S. border states of Texas and Arizona, one can purchase AK-47 and AR-15 machine guns, 9mm handguns, and even Barrett .50-caliber rifles in an over-the-counter cash transaction. Calderón's "drug war" has apparently created a boom for the 7,000 or so legal mom-and-pop gun stores in the U.S.-Mexican border region. According to a report published by the University of San Diego's Trans-Border Institute and the Mexico Institute at the Woodrow Wilson International Center for Scholars, the Mexican government's seizures of illegal firearms more than tripled between 2007 and 2008, from 9,553 to 29,824. The *Washington Post* reported in September 2010 that 62,800 of the more than 80,000 illegal guns confiscated between December 2006 and February 2010 were traced back to gun stores in the United States. (In 2008, U.S, agents confiscated only 70 guns at border crossings.) And those are just the guns found and reported by Mexican police and soldiers. In January 2011, the Brady Center to Prevent Gun Violence released a report using data from the Bureau of Alcohol, Tobacco, Firearms and Explosives (ATF) to show that since 2008 more than 62,000 firearms have "gone missing" from U.S. gun store inventories. Since the ATF only inspects 20 percent of gun stores, the number is most likely much higher. Similarly, the number of weapons seized, traced, and reported by Mexican authorities is surely only a fraction of all those guns still in use. The National Rifle Association says that Mexican drug gangs get their weapons from Central American arms traffickers and army deserters who take their guns with them. While that is not disputed, the number of guns seized in Mexico and traced back to legal U.S. dealers is staggering. Wherever they come from, all these machine guns and automatic pistols make up another booming side industry made possible by the murder spree in Mexico. Ironically, Calderón often blames U.S. gun laws and the easy availability in the United States for the violence in Mexico. (U.S. laws are largely to blame, but not the gun laws.)

Illegality also requires that one back up the moral discourse of prohibition with massive infusions of funds into armies and law-enforcement agencies. These infusions in turn require the production of arrests and drug seizures. Competitors in the drug economy use this need as a way to eliminate opponents and rivals, tipping off federal authorities to the whereabouts of one's enemy's stash and bedroom.

And in this context, illegality leads to a third complication: all disputes within the industry must be settled outside the law. The most popular method of conflict resolution in an illegal business culture where cash is so abundant as to be a kind of burden is contract murder. Betray, snitch, steal, mess up, forget, offend the boss, or say too much, and your transgression will likely lead to your death. The rule makers of the drug business do not impose fines, jail time, or community service, just death. And death is also good business. The Brookings Institution estimates that on average two thousand guns—ranging from cop-killer pistols to AK-47 and AR-15 assault rifles—are legally purchased in the United States and then smuggled across the border into Mexico *every day*.

This is what you cannot say: death is a part of the overhead, a business expense in a multibillion-dollar transnational illegal industry; the Mexican army and federal police are on the take, waging a war of extermination against suspected drug dealers and traffickers aligned with organizations that the federal government considers unruly or threatening, principally the Beltrán Leyva gang and the Zetas. That war of extermination provides cover for political assassinations, paramilitary executions, vigilante justice, and everyday extortion, abduction, and murder. That war of extermination has also fueled a coordinated, armed, and indescribably cruel counter-wave of murder as the Beltrán Leyva, Familia Michoacana and Zetas cartels scramble to maintain control of their territory and trafficking routes.

Death is everywhere.

In Ciudad Juárez, Francisco María Sagredo Villarreal, 69 years old, got tired of finding dead bodies discarded outside of his house. One day in November 2006, he nailed up a sign that read: PROHIBITED: LITTERING AND DUMPING CORPSES. He denounced the roaming bands of killers terrorizing the city and the complete impunity with which they always commit their crimes. He would find four more destroyed bodies there until October 2008 when a group of men shot Sagredo on his doorstep a little before noon. Two months later armed men killed his daughter Cinthia Sagredo Escobedo and dumped her body under the sign. The following day a group of men fired some twenty AK-47 bullets into his other daughter, Ruth Sagredo Escobedo, and a friend of hers as they drove in Cinthia's funeral procession. Both died.

The headlines assault. *El Universal*, July 25, 2010: "A Total of 70 Bodies Found in Narcograves in Nuevo León." *CNN México*, June 11, 2010: "Armed Group Kills 19 Inmates at Rehabilitation Center in Chihuahua." *Milenio*, May 1, 2010: "55 Thousand Pesos to Kill a Family." *Notimex*, April, 9, 2010: "Two Bodies Found Hanging from a Bridge in Cuernavaca." *La Jornada*, March 29, 2010: "10 Youths Between 13 and 19 Years Old Executed in Mountains of Durango." *New York Times*, February 2, 2010: "Gunmen in Mexico Kill 15 in Attack on a Teenagers' Party." *Associated Press*, January 8, 2010: "Mexico Cartel Stitches Rival's Face on Soccer Ball."

Of the 22,000 executions carried out between December 2006 and April 2010, the Mexican federal attorney general's office (Procuraduría General de la República, or PGR) had investigated 1,200 cases. Meaning the Mexican government did *not* investigate 95 percent of the drug war murders. (By May 2011, the known death toll had reached over 38,000 people, and the dismal level of arrests and convictions stayed the same. Some 30,000 murders were not even under investigation, their perpetrators thus guaranteed impunity.) The Mexican national daily *El Universal* first reported this story on June 21, 2010, after the 22,000 number became part of the public record in the Mexican Senate. The story quotes Jorge Chabat, a well-known drug-trafficking analyst and professor at the nonprofit Center for Economic Research and Teaching in Mexico City. Chabat says, "The small number of serious homicide cases being investigated by the PGR is a reflection of the incapacity to investigate those crimes." Incapacity? Ninety-five percent is too overwhelming a number to reflect incapacity. Ninety-five percent indicates an astonishing success rate, where the objective is not justice, but impunity.

Federal police make scores of arrests across the country every day. Those arrests lead to a minuscule number of convictions. According to Mexican federal reports analyzed by the investigative newsmagazine *ContraLínea*, of the 121,199 people that soldiers and police had detained in three and a half years of Calderón's war, prosecutors brought charges against only 1,306 for having links to one of the eight cartels presumed to operate in Mexico. Judges sentenced 735 to prison for organized crime. In 2009, federal police arrested, amidst great fanfare, eleven mayors and twenty-four other officials in Michoacán state for alleged links to drug traffickers. By late September 2010, prosecutors dropped the cases and judges ordered all but one set free for lack of evidence. The mayors and officials all belonged to the opposition Party of the Democratic Revolution (PRD) and had been arrested six weeks before the midterm federal elections. In the drug war, detentions and arrests produce results on the television screen, not in the courtroom.

And this is what they tell us: if you are found dead, shot through the face, wrapped in a soiled blanket, and left on some desolate roadside, then you are somehow to blame. You must have been into something bad to end up like that. Surely you were a drug dealer, a drug trafficker, or an official on the take. The very fact of your execution is the judgment against you, the determination of your guilt.

Mexican political cartoonist Antonio Helguera published a drawing in *La Jornada*, in March 2010, that captures this official logic of death in Mexico's and the United States' drug war. The title of the cartoon is *Morir en México*, To Die in Mexico. Eight asymmetrically aligned gravestones fill the frame and read, clockwise from the left: "She must have been into something; It was a gang feud; They murdered amongst themselves; What was he doing at that hour?; It was a settling of accounts; She dressed provocatively; Who knows what he was getting into; She was a whore."

The official logic of death seeks to safeguard the legitimacy of the army and federal police, and through them Calderón and his enforcers, to cloak them in a layer of discursive Kevlar that deflects all scrutiny. In the drug war, the dead are guilty, ipso facto, of their own murder. And whosoever would seek to argue otherwise confronts the likelihood of looking, briefly, at an AK-47.

But the drug war death squads make mistakes. And names wait with the dead.

ONE SHOULD NOT FORGET that the United States invaded Mexico in 1846 and conquered half of its national territory. Mexicans do not forget this; many in the United States never learn it.

The United States later invaded the port of Veracruz in 1914 during the Mexican Revolution to aid Venustiano Carranza in his war against Pancho Villa's Northern Division and Emiliano Zapata's Liberation Army of the South. U.S. intervention in Mexico is simultaneously a grounded historical fear-and-loathing in the population; a rhetorical device employed by all sectors of the political class to rally nationalist sentiment; and a brutish daily fact of Mexican life. The North American Free Trade Agreement and the drug war are examples of the latter.

The blood and chaos that accompany drug trafficking from Mexico into the United States are inextricably related to the simultaneous demand within the U.S. population for the classic illegal products one can use to get high or seek oblivion, and the insistence of U.S. politicians on an ideological commitment to prohibition that seeks to veil prohibition's use for social control.

Social control? Might that be exaggerating, or conspiracy theorizing? Civil rights advocate and litigator Michelle Alexander recently published a study of the drug war's impact on people of color, particularly African Americans, called *The New Jim Crow: Mass Incarceration in the Age of Colorblindness*. She argues that slavery evolved through Reconstruction into a caste system based on racial discrimination that in turn evolved during the era of the Civil Rights Movement and beyond into the drug war politics of mass incarceration of people of color. "We have not ended racial caste in America; we have merely redesigned it," Alexander writes. Felony convictions, she reminds us, open the door for all manner of legal discrimination: denial of the right to vote, serve on a jury, or access public education benefits; subjection to employment and housing discrimination. "Quite belatedly," Alexander writes, "I came to see that mass incarceration in the United States had, in fact, emerged as a stunningly comprehensive and well-designed system of racialized social control that functions in a manner similar to Jim Crow." That emergence came through the drug war.

President Ronald Reagan declared his War on Drugs in February 1982, a time when drug use in the United States was in decline, prisons seemed to be on their way out, Miami was awash in cocaine money and blood, and Central America was in the throes of left-wing revolutions. The drug war would radically alter all of that. Between 1980 and 2005, the number of people in U.S. prisons and jails on drug charges increased by 1,100 percent. By 2010 there were 2 million people in prisons and jails across the country. The United States now has the highest rate of incarceration of any nation in the world. In 2009, Marc Mauer of the Sentencing Project wrote, "The number of people incarcerated for a drug offense is now greater than the number incarcerated for *all* [other]offenses in 1980." And how is this a racialized form of social control? Again, according to the Sentencing Project, African Americans alone make up 14 percent of regular drug users and 56 percent of persons in state prison for drug offenses; African Americans serve almost as much time in federal prison for drug offenses (58.7 months) as whites do for violent offenses (61.7 months). More African Americans are behind bars now than were enslaved in 1850. In addition to racial profiling on the street, for twenty years possession of five grams of crack carried a mandatory five-year prison sentence; there was a 100:1 crack-to-powder-cocaine sentencing disparity, meaning that it took possession of 100 grams of white powder cocaine to require the same mandatory minimum sentence as possession of one gram of crack. (This law was revised on August 3, 2010, to require possession of 28 grams of crack to trigger the mandatory five-year sentence.)

The use of prohibition for racialized social control is the genesis of the modern drug-prohibition era. The first drug-prohibition law ever passed was an 1875 city ordinance in San Francisco banning opium, and with it, criminalizing working-class Chinese immigrants and attacking their local economy. The law came after more than two decades of discriminatory laws passed in California against Chinese workers, and six years before the 1882 Chinese Exclusion Act. The drug war has its deepest roots in racism.

In 1900, people in the United States could purchase opium, morphine, heroin, marijuana, and cocaine over the counter at drugstores or direct from producers through mail-order catalogues. Within twenty years that would change. Even though upper-class whites consumed opiates, cocaine, and marijuana, the prohibitionist fervor linked each drug with working-class people of color: opiates with Chinese, cocaine with African Americans, and marijuana with Mexicans. Historian Richard Davenport-Hines writes in *The Pursuit of Oblivion: A Global History of Narcotics*, "The fantasy of cocainised blacks from plantations and construction sites going on sexual rampages among white women soon raised a racist panic. A writer in the *Medical Record*, for example, warned that 'hitherto inoffensive, law-abiding negroes' were transformed by cocaine into a 'constant menace' whose 'sexual desires are increased and perverted.'"

The 1914 Harrison Act required registration, taxation, and medical prescription for most drugs. The 1919 Volstead Act inaugurated the Prohibition Era that included alcohol and lasted until 1933. Harry Anslinger was the first ever U.S. "drug czar" and ran the Federal Bureau of

Narcotics from 1930 to 1962. Anslinger pushed for and
defended the criminalization of marijuana from 1937 on
with disinformation, lies, and bullying. He accused medical
researchers who published a report finding that marijuana
use "does not lead to any physical, mental, or moral de-
generation," of being, "unsavory persons engaged in the
illicit marijuana trade" (quoted in *The Pursuit of Oblivion*).
Anslinger's tenor coincided with perhaps the first instance
of the Central Intelligence Agency knowingly funding and
arming drug traffickers, in this case Corsican gangs, to attack trade unionists and communists organizing among
dockworkers in Marseille.

In the 1950s and '60s, millions of Americans ex-
perimented with drugs. Vibrant countercultures emerged
within a broader movement of discarding the norms and
mores of a rigid, racist, and oppressive society. Those of the
dominant culture responded by further demonizing drug
use, conflating all forms of protest against racism and the
Vietnam War with criminality—drug use—and launched
the so-called War on Drugs.

Two months after taking office, Richard Nixon set up
the Special Presidential Task Force Relating to Narcotics,
Marijuana and Dangerous Drugs. The task force, in a June
6, 1969, report, said that Mexicans were "responsible for the
marijuana and drug abuse problem." The task force recom-
mended that Mexico "be forced into a program of defoliation
of the marijuana plants." How to force them? Kate Doyle of
the National Security Archive, put it this way, "The weapon

used to bludgeon Mexico into compliance would be a massive surprise attack on Mexico's border by U.S. law-enforcement personnel, code named 'Operation Intercept.'"

On September 21, 1969, Nixon launched Operation Intercept. The plan was simple; rigorously inspect every person, car, and plane arriving in the southern United States from Mexico. This virtually shut down the 1,969-mile border. Nixon did not inform Mexican President Gustavo Díaz Ordaz—who oversaw the army massacre of hundreds of students in Tlatelolco Plaza on October 2, 1968—of his plans. The unilateral decision incensed Mexican officials. The border traffic jams and the economic threat to Mexican exporters brought the Mexican government quickly to unequal and unfavorable negotiations. Mexico dispatched a delegation to Washington. and by October 10, the Díaz Ordaz administration had "convinced" the Nixon Administration to call off Operation Intercept, while the Nixon administration "convinced" their Mexican counterparts to join Operation Cooperation and through it the United States' War on Drugs—a term Nixon used publicly for the first time on June 17, 1971.

Seven years after Operation Intercept, in September 1976, the Mexican government launched a military defoliation program called Operation Condor. Five thousand soldiers and 350 federal police, working together with thirty U.S. Drug Enforcement Agency (DEA) agents stationed in Mexico and using forty airplanes—some from the United States—attacked and destroyed tens of thousands of acres of marijuana fields in Sinaloa, Chihuahua, Durango, and Guerrero.

At that time there were no known transnational drug cartels in Mexico. The relatively small marijuana growers and traffickers in Sinaloa, however, fled Operation Condor and relocated in cities across the country. Operation Condor burned marijuana fields, but it also prompted the geographical dispersion of marijuana growers and traffickers from the rugged, isolated mountains of Sinaloa to the cities of Guadalajara, Tijuana, and Ciudad Juárez. Also, as soon as the Operation Condor soldiers went away, people replanted the burned fields.

Before Operation Condor, Sinaloans grew marijuana in Sinaloa and smuggled it into the United States. After Operation Condor Sinaloans grew marijuana in Sinaloa, Sonora, Chihuahua, Guerrero, Michoacán, Jalisco, Durango, Zacatecas, and Baja California and smuggled it into the United States. Sinaloans controlled every major drug-trafficking organization that grew throughout the 1980s. Sinaloans would run the Guadalajara Cartel, the Tijuana Cartel, the Juárez Cartel, and, of course, the Sinaloa Cartel. The Gulf Cartel burst onto the scene in the early '90s with the rise of Carlos Salinas and the passage of the North American Free Trade Agreement (NAFTA). La Familia Michoacana would declare its independence in 2006 and be all but dismantled by January 2011.

Cocaine money built Miami in the 1970s, but by the early 1980s, the blood in the streets got to be too much—

homicides in Miami went from 104 in 1976 to 621 in 1981—
so the U.S. government decided to push the gunplay out.
Enter Reagan and *his* War on Drugs. The Reagan administration shut off the direct trafficking routes from Colombia
and the Caribbean into Florida with a massive deployment
of federal agents. The drugs kept coming. No Miami nightclub went without blow. The Colombian cocaine smugglers
looked to Mexico and its long and desolate border with the
United States. Thanks to Operation Condor, the Mexican
marijuana traffickers from Sinaloa had built networks along
the length of the border for marijuana smuggling. The pot
kept coming, more than ever, and now with cocaine from
Colombia.

Reagan's drug war consolidated the racist under-
pinnings of prohibition into a new racial caste system,
as Michelle Alexander argues. It also expanded upon the
U.S. hemispheric "security" policy—or counterinsurgency
proxy wars—and its unsavory drug habit. It has been well
documented in books like Alfred McCoy's *The Politics of
Heroin: CIA Complicity in the Global Drug Trade* that the
Central Intelligence Agency was involved in trafficking
narcotics in Southeast Asia throughout the 1950s and '60s
and in Afghanistan and Central America in the 1970s and
'80s to fund anti-communist death squads. Throughout the
1980s the CIA also supported counterinsurgency wars in
Nicaragua funded from cocaine smuggling. Robert Parry
and Brian Barger were the first reporters to break the story
for the Associated Press in 1985. Reagan administration

officials launched a personal defamation campaign against both reporters and drove them out of the AP. From April 1986 to April 1989, the U.S. Senate Subcommittee on Narcotics and Terrorism held hearings and investigated the allegations of CIA involvement in supporting counterinsurgency forces in Nicaragua involved in cocaine trafficking to the United States.

The Subcommittee report, released on April 13, 1989, found, among other things, "involvement in narcotics trafficking by individuals associated with the Contra movement" and "payments to drug traffickers by the U.S. State Department of funds authorized by the Congress for humanitarian assistance to the Contras, in some cases after the traffickers had been indicted by federal law-enforcement agencies on drug charges, in others while traffickers were under active investigation by these same agencies." The three main newspapers in the United States buried short articles in their back pages: *Washington Post*, page A20; *Los Angeles Times*, page A11; *New York Times*, page A8. Peter Kornbluh of the National Security Archive wrote in the *Columbia Journalism Review* that "the Kerry Committee report was relegated to oblivion; and opportunities were lost to pursue leads, address the obstruction from the CIA and the Justice Department that Senate investigators say they encountered, and both inform the public and lay the issue to rest." Reagan administration officials mocked the Subcommittee chair, Senator John Kerry, and the media followed suit; *Newsweek* famously called Kerry a "randy conspiracy buff."

In July 1995, after publishing an award-winning exposé of California's drug asset forfeiture laws the year before called "The Forfeiture Racket," investigative reporter Gary Webb, then at the *San Jose Mercury News*, picked up a lead on the CIA, the Contras, and cocaine trafficking to Los Angeles and decided to follow the story. His articles reported that the CIA had supported known drug traffickers in Nicaragua, but for the first time it also traced the arrival of those drugs in the form of crack cocaine to African American neighborhoods in South Central Los Angeles. Webb published his series, "The Dark Alliance," in mid-August 1996 and came face to face with the hired guns of silence. The same three newspapers that ignored the Kerry Committee Report in 1989 (*Washington Post*, *Los Angeles Times*, *New York Times*) assigned teams of experienced investigative reporters and collectively published more than 30,000 words—*not* to follow the story that Gary Webb broke, but to break Gary Webb. One of the *Washington Post* reporters assigned to debunk "Dark Alliance" was Walter Pincus, who spied on youth groups for the CIA in the late '50s and early '60s.

Nick Schou, in his book *Kill the Messenger: How the CIA's Crack-Cocaine Controversy Destroyed Journalist Gary Webb*, describes how the *Washington Post*, *Los Angeles Times*, and *New York Times* hit pieces hooked onto contradictions in testimony by convicted drug felons cited in "Dark Alliance" to bludgeon the credibility of Webb and the *San Jose Mercury News*, pressuring the paper to retract the story and demote Webb; the editors sent him off to cover the daily beat in Cupertino. He resigned soon after. Discredited and unable to get a job at a newspaper, he worked for the California Senate, then briefly for the *Sacramento News and Review* before shooting himself in the head with a .38 on December 10, 2004.

In 1998, only days after the *San Jose Mercury News* announced Webb's resignation, the CIA published a statement vindicating the agency of collaboration with drug dealers. A month later the CIA released the first volume of a report supporting that claim. A few months later the CIA released the second volume of the report, contradicting what agents had previously said and written, and admitting that between 1982 and 1995 its agents worked with known drug traffickers supporting the Contras and had maintained an agreement with the Justice Department to not report drug dealing by its "assets." There was no scandal, there was no outcry. The major papers did not assign teams of investigative reporters to probe further into the prior twelve years of CIA lies and complicity in drug trafficking. Silence.

One does not need to talk of conspiracy theories or even conspiracies; the acknowledged facts are poignant enough. One does not need to ponder the possible plans or intentions of Ronald Reagan and his administration officials with the 1982 declaration of war. Thirty years later mass incarceration through drug laws has become the new Jim Crow caste system of racial discrimination in the United States, and the murder and chaos that always accompany

illegal drug trafficking have been pushed over the border
into Mexico.

If there were really a war on drugs, the drugs would be
winning: the 2009 U.S. National Survey on Drug Use and
Health estimated that 21.8 million people aged twelve or
older had consumed an illicit drug within the past month.
The United Nations Office on Drugs and Crime ventured
a guess in its 2009 *World Drug Report* that between 170 million and 250 million people use illicit drugs worldwide.
The United States is the world's largest consumer of every
drug on the market. In 2009, more people in the United
States got blasted than any year prior, while 2009 was also
the bloodiest year then on record in Mexico's drug war. The
direct correlation between U.S. recreational drug use, prohibition, and the murder and terror unleashed throughout
Mexico cannot be avoided. Some drugs may cause harm, but
prohibition kills.

With full support from the U.S. Congress, successive
presidential administrations have used drug war programs
such as extradition and the annual certification reviews
that threaten loss of foreign aid and sanctions for decerti-
fied countries as tools to bend less powerful nations into
compliance with prohibition and U.S. intervention. As
Richard Davenport-Hines writes in *The Pursuit of Oblivion*,
"Prohibition policies have turned licit, if dangerous, medi-
cines into the world's most lucrative and tightly organized
black market. Essentially prohibition has been a technique
of informal American cultural colonisation."

DEATH IS ESSENTIAL IN MEXICO. Troubled, fractured, be-
leaguered, and contested, like the nation itself, representations of death are an inextricable feature of Mexican daily
life, popular culture, and national identity.

Take Day of the Dead, November 2, when the souls
of the dead visit and family and friends honor them with
their favorite foods and candlelit altars. In some regions, like
communities in parts of Oaxaca, Day of the Dead is the most
important spiritual day of the year. The celebrations are national events that draw the participation of millions. The
rituals have also become prime attractions for international
tourists as a singularly Mexican experience. Mexicans and
Chicanos in the United States hold Day of the Dead ceremonies as acts of affirmation of Mexican national pride and
cultural identity. The dominant image in Day of the Dead
sculptures, offerings, and art is the skull, especially the ed-
ible sugar skulls elaborately decorated in the brightest hues.

Then there is *la nota roja*, the crime beat or blood
news, an entire newspaper industry built on publishing
daily, gruesome front-page photographs of the newly dead:
car accidents, stabbings, beatings, and recently, with great
frequency, executions. In Mexico City and other cities,
newsstand sellers string these papers up at intersections
where pedestrians gather and gawk throughout the day. In
some small towns, distribution amounts to someone driving through city streets in a Volkswagen Beetle with mega-
phones mounted on the roof, blaring enticements with a
vendor's rehearsed excitement, shouting calls like this one I

once heard in Tlapa, Guerrero, "*¡Mira la sangriente muerte que tuvo!*" ("See how bloody her death was!")

One of the most immediately recognizable icons of Mexican popular art is the skeleton. The engraver Jose Guadalupe Posada (1852–1913) used skulls and skeletons both to mock the Mexican elite during the Porfirio Díaz dictatorship and to celebrate popular traditions like the fandango. Posada influenced Mexico's famed muralists Diego Rivera and José Clemente Orozco, who also deployed skeletons in their otherwise social realist murals. In Posada's work, like the Day of the Dead sugar skulls, images of death are at times festive, at times ironic, but never gruesome.

Mexico's most celebrated novel, Juan Rulfo's *Pedro Páramo*, takes place in a village of the dead. The protagonist, Juan Preciado, promises his dying mother that he will seek out his father, Pedro Páramo, in Comala. His father has been dead for years, murdered by an unrecognized son to whom he had refused to give money to pay for the burial of the son's dead wife. Preciado himself dies as he grasps the truth of Comala: everyone there, all the people he has met and spoken with, those from whom he has learned the story of his father's life and death, everyone there is dead.

Thousands of people across Mexico worship, *La Santa Muerte*, Holy Death. Some pray that she take care of relatives making the trek across the Arizona desert to look for work or return to jobs they've held for years. Some pray that she protect relatives in prison. Some pray that she ward off violence. Some pray that she help them on college entrance exams.

Some pray for jobs, luck, or love. Many tattoo her image on their chests, shoulders, or backs. The tall, gaunt skeleton, robed in black or white or red, holds the world, or a scythe, or a scale, or some combination of them in her hands.

And while La Santa Muerte is famed as the patron saint of killers, drug lords, and thieves, a visit to one of her main altars in Mexico gives a different impression. One July day in 2010, I spoke with Enriqueta Romero Romero, who tends La Santa Muerte's altar in the Mexico City tough, working class barrio of Tepito. Romero speaks of death and La Santa Muerte with reverence and tenderness. "Death has always existed," she said, "it is something beautiful about life, that we are born and we die." She calls La Santa Muerte *mi doña flaquita* (roughly, "my dear skinny lady") and smiles wide when her visitors use the same name. While we were talking one of her daughters dropped by with her newborn, and Romero whisked the little baby into her arms and held her up, kissing her and holding her up again, saying, "my little princess, precious little thing." The feeling at Romero's altar to La Santa Muerte in Tepito was one of sweetness.

When Emily Rodríguez, a 28-year-old public servant in Mexico City's district attorney's office, came up to buy a Santa Muerte candle, she was wearing blue jeans and a black SANTA MUERTE T-shirt. She visits every year on Day of the Dead and leaves a bottle of brandy for La Santa Muerte. She also has a small altar at home where she prays daily. I asked her why she believes in La Santa Muerte. "When you look in her eyes, well, she doesn't exactly have eyes, but if you look in her cavities, she inspires trust," Emily said. "In our pre-Hispanic culture we had our gods of death. We feel like death is a part of life, there is no reason to satanize it." I asked her about the culture of drug gangs and gunmen who proclaim belief in La Santa Muerte. "If you use *La Santísima Muerte* [Most Holy Death] for bad things, they'll come back to haunt you," she said. For her, La Santa Muerte embodies trust, not murder. "She inspires trust in me and that's why I believe in La Santísima Muerte. I personally don't believe in people who become saints; I don't believe in that. But death is certain."

A visit to the altar of La Santa Muerte offers some insight into particularly Mexican feelings about death, but nothing here could help one explain the wicked cruelty of drug war murder.

"During Mexico's twentieth century," anthropologist Claudio Lomnitz writes in his book *Death and the Idea of Mexico*, "a gay familiarity with death became a cornerstone of national identity."

"The nationalization of an ironic intimacy with death is a singularly Mexican strategy," Lomnitz notes, and its roots in Mexican social history are deep: "The cult of death could be thought of as the oldest, seminal, and most authentic element of Mexico's popular culture."

Mexican death symbolism, Lomnitz argues, reflects differences between strong and weak states, imperial and post-colonial states, and that Mexico's place in that difference is unique: "As the largest and richest of Spain's New

World colonies, Mexico at independence had real imperial aspirations. As the United States' next-door neighbor, it was the first to become the booty of that republic."

Lomnitz continues: "If death has become a looming presence in Mexican political discourse, it is because the political control over dying, the dead, and representations of the dead and the afterlife has been key to the formation of the modern state, images of popular culture, and a properly national modernity."

If "the political control over dying . . . has been key to the formation of the modern state," what does the explosion of vicious, uncontrolled murder say about the contemporary Mexican state? What does the state's unofficial authorship of so much of that murder say? If it says that the state is somehow weak, where does the fracture lie? Or, we might ask, what is the nature of the injury or ailment that causes this weakness?

And yet for all the cultural depth and uniqueness in attitudes, representations, and rituals of death in Mexico, it would be a mistake to look exclusively into Mexican history and culture to explain the particularly cruel and gruesome character or the increasing prevalence of drugland executions in Mexico.

"Any attempt to view it all with uniquely Mexican roots, rather than as part of something horizontal, global, is in error," Claudio Lomnitz told me one afternoon in Mexico City. "In analyzing the forms of narco violence, Mexican history is not irrelevant, but it is necessary to know where it is relevant. Narco violence is related to other forms of violence and also influences them; the narcos import, but they also export. There is a dimension that is in dialogue with a globalized culture."

The Zetas, widely considered the most spectacular, brazen, and heinous of all the hit men working in the narcotics marketplace, serve as a perfect example of Lomnitz's point. The Zeta assassins first studied counterinsurgency strategies in the United States and Israel as part of the Mexican Special Forces. They also hired Guatemalan Special Forces soldiers known as Kaibiles—an institution that received decades of training in counterinsurgency tactics from the United States army—to serve in their ranks. The Zetas adopted Al Qaeda's practice of video recording beheadings and posting the footage on YouTube. Other cartel assassins across Mexico soon followed their example.

It is an error to think that Mexico is either the principal location of or an isolated battlefield in the fiercely competitive global marketplace for illegal narcotics. Just like the trafficking of the drugs themselves and the prohibition policies against them, the drug market is transnational. Mexico's current position in the so-called drug war can only be understood in a global context, taken together with the countries from which certain drugs originate and those where most drugs get sold to users and consumed, namely Colombia and Peru on the one hand, and the United States on the other, but also countries as far from Mexico as Argentina and Australia. Wherever drugs are banned by law and also grown, shipped, sold, smoked, swallowed, snorted, or injected the drug war zone extends its reach.[1]

In the logic of the drug war, to die in Mexico is to be guilty of your own death. But, the bare facts—when they can be rescued from oblivion—shatter the sordid drug war myths of cops and robbers, of Robin Hood drug lords, of an honest United States of America and a corrupt Mexico. Through the stories of the dead and those who resist the laws of silence, we may begin to approach an understanding of the killings and look for a way out.

NOTE

1. I take the term "drug war zone," from Howard Campbell, professor of anthropology at the University of Texas at El Paso, who defines the zone as "the transnational, fluid cultural space in which contending forces battle over the meaning, value, and control of drugs."

Campbell's 2009 book *Drug War Zone: Frontline Dispatches from the Streets of El Paso and Juárez* contains in-depth interviews with direct participants in what is now the bloodiest corner of the global drug war zone. Campbell speaks with retailers, wholesalers, smugglers, police, consumers, and witnesses to executions, all from varying backgrounds and life experiences. His introduction provides lucid definitions of several key concepts in the drug war zone, rare clarity that is useful in stepping into a world where, as Campbell writes, "The conflict is waged sometimes in the open, but more often in a clandestine, subterranean world, a social space in which truth is elusive and relative and in which paranoia, fear, and mystery are the orders of the day."

First, consider the notion of "drug trafficking" itself, which, Campbell writes, "is an illegal form of capitalist accumulation. In some cases, it is an almost caricatured celebration of consumerism and wealth . . . facilitated by neoliberalism and collusion with elements of the state. . . . I argue that ultimately the drug trade is part of the U.S.

and Mexican economic systems." This should not come as much of a shock, but it is useful to keep at hand as a simple, clear definition of a complex and purposefully obfuscated transnational phenomenon.

Campbell also provides very helpful descriptions—worth quoting at length—of two central and little understood drug war categories: cartels and their special breed of territorial control. Drug cartels, he writes, should be thought of as "shifting, contingent, temporal alliances of traffickers whose territories and memberships evolve and change because of conflicts, imprisonment, deaths, changing political circumstances, etc., and whose fortunes and strengths wax or wane or die out over time. . . . Moreover, many of the functions of a cartel are in fact carried out by cells, which are groups of outsourced growers, packagers, drivers, warehouse guards, gunmen, street sellers, etc., who have little or no connection to the larger drug organization . . . and whose services are bought and paid for with cash or drugs."

To grasp the phenomenal success of Mexican drug-trafficking organizations in moving their product, gathering cash payments, and depositing billions of U.S. dollars in illicit cash into the legal economy in spite of a multinational war against them, one must establish a clear understanding of the concept of the *plaza*. Campbell's succinct, general description of this fundamental drug war concept is excellent.

"Transportation routes and territories controlled by specific cartels in collusion with police, military, and government officials," writes Campbell, "are known as *plazas*. Control of a *plaza* gives the drug lord and police commander of an area the power to charge less-powerful traffickers tolls, known as *pisos*. Generally, one main cartel dominates a *plaza* at any given time, although this control is often contested or subverted by internal conflict, may be disputed among several groups, and is subject to rapid change. Attempts by rival cartels to ship drugs through a *plaza* or take over a *plaza* controlled by their enemies [have] led to much of the recent violence in Mexico. The cartel that has the most power in a particular *plaza* receives police or military protections for its drug shipments. Authorities provide official documentation for loaded airplanes, freight trucks, and cars and allow traffickers to pass freely through airports and landing strips, freeway toll roads and desert highways, and checkpoints and border crossings.

"Typically, a cartel purchases the loyalty of the head of the federal police or the military commander in a particular district. This official provides officers or soldiers to physically protect drug loads in transit or in storage facilities, and in some cases to serve as bodyguards to high-level cartel members. Police on the cartel payroll intimidate, kidnap, or murder opponents of the organization, although they may also extort larger payments from the cartel with which they are associated. Additionally cartel members establish relationships [or] connections with state governors or mayors of major cities, high-ranking officials in federal law enforcement, military and naval officers and commanders and other powerful politicians and bureaucrats. These national connections facilitate the use of transportation routes and control of a given *plaza*. In addition to large-scale international smuggling, cartels distribute huge quantities of drugs for domestic consumption."

TWO

Let the atrocious images haunt us. Even if they are only tokens and cannot possibly encompass most of the reality to which they refer; they still perform a vital function. The images say: This is what human beings are capable of doing—may volunteer to do, enthusiastically, self-righteously. Don't forget.

—Susan Sontag

ERNESTO MARTÍNEZ, KNOWN AS *PEPIS* (pronounced PAY-peace) is a tall, lanky, wisecracking 40-year-old who has been working the *nota roja* for thirteen years. He has seen more death than most morticians.

Primera Hora is a daily blood news tabloid based in Culiacán, Sinaloa, and published by the newspaper *Noroeste*, Culiacán's main broadsheet daily. The *Primera Hora* newsroom is a small windowless box with five computers, a few filing cabinets, and a powerful air conditioner. To get here you must go around to the back of the *Noroeste* building, pass through a security checkpoint, and walk down a long hall in what appears to be a desolate storage basement. When

I arrive at five in the afternoon, Pepis, a staff photographer and writer says, "Welcome to the bunker."

Pepis introduces me to the afternoon shift at *Primera Hora*: Marco Santos, the editor, and Juan Carlos Cruz, a staff writer and sometimes photographer. They all wear white button-down shirts with the *Primera Hora* logo stitched across the chest. Pepis then tells me that about an hour earlier there was a *levantón*, or "a pick-up," that special type of kidnapping in Mexico that leads inevitably to execution. Several reporters and local police arrived on the scene soon after. As they did, however, the gunmen came back to grab someone else. They walked up to the reporters, aimed their assault rifles in their faces, and said, "Don't take any pictures, and be very careful not to publish anything." The police of course did nothing, and the gunmen apparently did not even feel the need to warn them against pursuing them. Pepis sympathizes with the local cop's plight in such situations: "The police only had pistols, and the gunmen all carried AK-47s."

As we talk, representatives of the United Nations and the Organization of American States are getting ready to meet with a group of invited journalists to inquire about press freedom in Culiacán. I ask if any *Primera Hora* reporters will attend the meeting and Marco tells me that no one from the crime beat press corps was invited and he wouldn't want to go anyway. "Those meetings don't do anything, never lead to anything concrete," he says.

The censorship power of the cartels is inviolable, they

tell me. At *Primera Hora*, they try to avoid attracting cartel wrath altogether. Their job is now to count bodies and photograph and describe death scenes. On particularly bloody days the front page will include an "executometer," or *ejecutómetro*, showing the grim total.

"Investigative journalism is extinct here," Pepis says.

For example, if a group of drug assassins leaves a written message at a murder scene, *Primera Hora* will reference that a message was left but not publish in the article or the photograph the text of the message itself. This editorial decision was made by someone within the Sinaloa Cartel.

They tell me that a gunman killed a chef who prepared regional shellfish dishes for the Sinaloa Cartel boss Ismael "El Mayo" Zambada, also known as MZ. The killers left a message that read: THIS WILL HAPPEN TO ALL WHO WORK FOR MZ. *Primera Hora* published the text of the message in the news article that they posted online and got a call within minutes. The voice on the phone said, "Take that shit down!" Marco called the news director at *Noroeste* to confer. The director concurred: "Take it down and just mention that a message was left." And hence an editorial policy was born.

Pepis started at *Noroeste* as a member of the predawn crew that assembled the morning paper. After six months he began to work preparing the negatives and slides used in the printing process. At that time *Primera Hora* had a day-shift staff photographer who was famously lazy. Come lunchtime at 2:00 p.m. he would head out, turn off his mobile phone, and disappear until 6:00 p.m., leaving a four-hour chunk of

the day uncovered. Several of the crime beat reporters joked
with Pepis that he should learn photography so he could
cover the languid photographer's dead time. Pepis liked the
idea. With his savings he bought a 1970s Yashica 35mm
camera and studied darkroom developing techniques, how
to work the camera, and finally the craft of taking pictures.
He then apprenticed for a year, unpaid, covering the unofficial 2:00 p.m.–6:00 p.m. "lunch" shift before his night shift
at the paper's printing press. After a year, he started as a
crime beat staff photographer for *Primera Hora*.

I ask the *Primera Hora* team to walk me through the background to the current state of war. In 2001, El Chapo busts
out of federal, maximum-security prison to reclaim old territories, they tell me. At this time there was a grand alliance
between Sinaloan drug cartels called The Federation. This
alliance included the Arrellano Félix brothers (from Sinaloa,
but in control of the *plaza* in Tijuana), the Carrillo Fuentes
family (also from Sinaloa, but in control of the *plaza* in
Ciudad Juárez), and El Chapo and El Mayo Zambada (both
from Sinaloa and in control of the *plaza* in Sinaloa).

In 2004, assassins working for El Chapo gunned down
Rodolfillo Carrillo Fuentes—brother of Amado, "The Lord
of the Skies"—and his wife, Giovanna Quevedo Gastélum,
in front of a movie theater in Culiacán. The Carrillo Fuentes
gang sent a group of killers to murder El Chapo's brother Pablo. With these murders The Federation dissolved,
the alliances crumbled, and the war began. The violence

ebbed in 2005 and surged again in 2006. During this time El Chapo made an alliance with the Sinaloan Beltrán Leyva brothers: Arturo, Héctor, Alfredo, Mario, and Carlos. The Beltrán Leyva brothers recruited Edgar "La Barbie" Valdez from the rival Gulf Cartel, and together they became the main armed wing of the Sinaloa Cartel tasked with invading new territories, taking over and opening up new *plazas*. One of the first places they went was Acapulco, Guerrero, where two state police officers were decapitated and their severed heads impaled on a fence one morning in late April 2006.

In 2008, the alliance between El Chapo and El Mayo and the Beltrán Leyva brothers fell apart. El Chapo apparently tipped off federal authorities to the whereabouts of Alfredo "El Mochomo" Beltrán's safe house in Mexico City—where Alfredo was arrested on January 21, 2008—as a trade to secure the release of one of his sons from maximum-security prison in Mexico State. As a result, El Chapo's son Archibaldo Guzmán was released a few months later, on April 11. The Beltrán Leyva clan demanded their brother's release, and it seems that when El Chapo refused to help, they sent a hit squad to kill El Chapo's other son, Édgar, in the parking lot of a supermarket on May 9. On May 7 and 8, hand-painted narco-banners were hung in Sinaloa with messages like POLICE-SOLDIERS, SO THAT IT BE CLEAR, EL MOCHOMO STILL CARRIES WEIGHT. SINCERELY, ARTURO BELTRÁN. The war was on again. The Beltrán Leyva gang made alliances with El Chapo's bitter enemies the Carrillo Fuentes of the Juárez Cartel and the Zetas, then still working for the Gulf Cartel.

When I ask about Calderón and *his* war on drugs, the crime beat reporters urge the following distinction: there is the War on Drugs (*la Guerra del Narco*), and then there is the Drug War (*la Narcoguerra*). In the War on Drugs the federal government sends tens of thousands of soldiers and federal police parading through the streets, then announces the seizures of drugs and weapons and the arrests of alleged drug traffickers. In the Drug War, trafficking organizations—and the various local, state, and federal authorities allied with them—battle in the streets and seek to exterminate each other and establish absolute dominance in a given *plaza*. The two wars sometimes overlap, but they are not identical.

Pepis carries a radio similar to those used by the Red Cross and is able to intercept their communications. He has studied their codes. This is how he learns when and where the bodies fall. He used to tap into the police radio system, but the cops recently shifted to a prohibitively expensive Israeli radio company, and so now he taps into the ambulance radios.

As we are talking in the bunker, he picks up a call and holds the radio close to his ear. He hears, "five bravo fourteen," grabs his mobile phone and makes several calls to confirm. Five stands for wounded, bravo for bullet wound, and fourteen for dead. So "five bravo fourteen," translates to "the bullet wound victim died." That is his cue. Pepis looks up and says that someone has been executed on the outskirts of town. "It appears as if it is the guy they grabbed in front of the reporters an hour or two ago," he says.

We pile into the white Chevy pickup with the *Primera Hora* logo painted on the sides and head out. It takes us about fifteen minutes to get to the scene.

The pride of the blood photographer used to be arriving on the scene before the cops, paramedics, and most important, other reporters. The photographer could thus work in peace. He or she could walk right up to the body without navigating police lines and have a few minutes to try to get the right angle and capture the light without the image being filled with the clutter of detectives, ambulances, and other photographers. The photographer could fill the frame with death and nothing else, and hope for the front page and good sales. Not anymore. In too many occasions killers return to the scene of an execution to either make sure the victim is in fact dead, or to kill someone else they missed the first time. In such situations the killers will execute anyone in the way of their task. So now reporters, paramedics, and even the police themselves will often wait awhile before getting too close to a dead body on the street.

"Trying to get the exclusive shot is a thing of the past here for us," Pepis says. "We've had to put a stop to that, to self-censor. Now when there is an event, we'll go, but we try not to get there before the authorities."

The Culiacán government says that they have an average response time to homicide calls of four to eight minutes. Pepis says it is more like half an hour, and it can sometimes take them up to five hours. He gives an example, "I went to cover a homicide in Navolato once. . . . From the moment I heard the report, I coordinated with my colleagues and lost ten minutes. In the time it took me to drive to Navolato, another twenty-five minutes, so it's now been thirty-five minutes. I arrive at the scene and see a person's body discarded there, but there is nobody around. No one is there except the curious locals looking at the body. I asked one guy, 'Hey, the cops?' 'They haven't come yet,' he says. I was waiting around for another thirty minutes when we see several trucks with mounted headlights like the drug gunmen use, coming at us from the distance. And the trucks are going full speed, jumping over all the street bumps. The people scream, 'Here come the killers!' They dive for cover in the bush and run where they can. And the body is alone again, like a dead animal in the woods. I stayed nearby. The trucks belonged to the state police, arriving as fast as they could, putting on their circus, but over an hour had passed since the report went out."

We arrive at the scene and park the truck. The body has been discarded on the side of a dirt road a few feet from a barbed wire fence. Everything is green; it is the rainy season. We are at the northern edge of the city, about a hundred yards from the back wall of the last subdivision. Looking across a weed-covered field we can see clearly the second-story windows of at least ten houses. The people who live there must have heard the shots. No one would think of knocking on doors to ask them if they had: not the reporters, not the police. No one does this because the people in the houses would certainly tell you nothing, though there is always the chance that they would report your snooping around to people who drive around in SUVs with assault rifles.

We are the first reporters on the scene. There are two police trucks there already and the police are cordoning off the immediate vicinity around the body with yellow caution tape, tying it to a barbed wire fence, stretching it across the road and tying it to a tree on the other side. We duck under the fence and are able to get within feet of the body on that side. The photographers crouch and get to work.

I begin to write observations in my notebook when a young man walks up to me and asks, "Do you want the name?"

The young man did not ask if I wanted "his name," but rather "the name."

I say yes and he tells me: Juan Antonio González Zamorra. I say thank you.

The state forensic team arrives and starts to survey the scene.

Juan Antonio González's dead body is face down. His T-shirt has been pulled up over his head, tying up both of his arms in the shirt. On his left side where his shirt has been pulled up you can see two small circular wounds. One of the photographers comments, "The orifices are very small, close range, must have been a cop-killer," a 5.7x28mm-caliber pistol famed for its ability to pierce body armor. The T-shirt covering his head is filled with blood, still wet, seeping slowly through the fabric and into the ground.

I notice a man busily walking around the scene talking on a mobile phone. He is all business. He wears dress slacks and a button-down collared shirt both stitched with the word EMAUS. I glance back at the parked vehicles: one is a van with EMAUS painted in huge letters on the side.

The police take pictures of Juan Antonio González's dead body. The forensics team locates the bullet casings, notes the body's position, and measures the distances between the body and the casings. The news photographers walk the perimeter of the scene taking photographs of the police and forensics team working.

Everything about the scene is routine. Nothing here would lead you to believe that the form on the ground around which everyone's movements, everyone's tasks and actions and jobs are oriented, was once a person.

I walk up to the young man who offered to give me "the name" and strike up a conversation. His name is Jonathan and he works for the Moreh funeral parlor. "I'm the one who'll be preparing this guy's body in a bit," he says.

I ask about Emaus. They are also a funeral service Jonathan tells me, the competition. I ask how he found out about the body. Moreh has a police radio and monitors the frequency, just as Pepis monitors the Red Cross frequency. It turns out that the first people to arrive at the scene of an execution—a crime scene, one supposes—those who apparently have no fear of returning gunmen, are representatives of Culiacán's multimillion-dollar funeral parlors. They hear the calls go out on the police radios and rush to the scene. Once there, they will search the body for some form of identification and call the dead person's name back in to headquarters. The funeral parlor will then dispatch a crew to seek out the dead person's family. This crew arrives with "the bad news," as Jonathan puts it, but they soften it up with lies, "so that the family doesn't get too scared." They'll say, "We're really sorry, but we have information that your beloved was in an accident. We can take you to where it happened." On the drive the crew will explain that they work for the funeral parlor and will be ready and able to take care of the family's wake and burial needs.

"Every day there's work," Jonathan says. Indeed, proud of his employer, Jonathan tells me that Moreh was in charge of the funerals for such major capos and their relatives as Nacho Coronel, Arturo Beltrán, and El Chapo's son Édgar.

But, considering that the Beltrán Leyvas and El Chapo are sworn enemies whose feud generates all these dead bodies, isn't it dangerous to work for both sides, or either side, for that matter?

"They are very polite," he says of his customers, "and they tip well."

After some fifteen or twenty minutes the forensics team and the police lift the body into the forensics van and drive off. And with that, the official investigation into Juan Antonio González's murder is done.

We drive back to the bunker. Pepis drops us off at the back door and goes to park the truck. It is raining. We walk into

the office and sit down. Marco and Juan Carlos start typing;
I continue to write notes in my notebook. Less than five
minutes later Pepis bursts in and shouts, "Let's go!" Another
body has been dumped.

Juan Carlos writes the article about Juan Antonio
González's murder in less than ten minutes. Pepis downloads
his photographs and makes a selection to send off to the editors. First, however, he goes through each selected image and
digitally distorts the faces of the police, forensics workers,
and anyone else. He also distorts the license plates and squad
car numbers of any official vehicles that may appear in the
background. He saves the altered files and sends them on.

We head out again, this time to Navolato.

"Everything has become just counting the dead," Cruz
says as we walk out. "All investigative and feature stories
have been extinguished. We used to go out to villages and
talk with people. Not anymore. And it's not just here, it's all
across Mexico."

Cruz knows what he's talking about. He won the
Mexican National Journalism Award in 2002 for an in-depth
investigative feature on a massacre in the Sinaloan mountains. He knows that good reporting demands going places
and talking to people, and he knows that that has become
next to impossible, which is to say, potentially fatal.

"Narco has always been around," he says, "people
learned to live with it. As long as you didn't stick your nose
where it didn't belong. . . . But not anymore. It has become
a psychotic environment."

In the truck again I ask about Navolato. Since arriving in Culiacán I had seen daily reports of executions and shoot-outs in Navolato. I had heard that the entire municipal police force had quit en masse. It turned out, however, that there were still twelve acting officers, four on duty at any given time, for the entire municipality, an area of 882 square miles with a population of more than 135,000. Of course, the four on-duty police officers never leave the station. I asked several friends and contacts about going there, and every one of them had said the same thing: do not go there alone.

"Navolato was part of the Carrillos' territory," Juan Carlos says. "No one could go there without their permission. It is a strategic municipality, right next to Culiacán; it also includes coastline, good roads, and several landing strips. Navolato was untouchable. As soon as you entered the municipality there were cartel spies reporting on who was driving in. Now Navolato belongs to El Chapo."

And so, I ask, all the dead bodies discarded on roadsides in Navolato, one assumes that they were people accused of working for, or perhaps just being sympathetic or related to, the Carrillos, and their killers are El Chapo's gunmen? Do all these executions follow some logic of extermination?

Marco and Juan Carlos look at me, and then nod. "When a dead body is found no one says anything like that," Pepis says while driving. "We just publish that so and so was executed and that's it."

No one is able to protect them, they said, if they were to publish anything that disgruntles a cartel. But, I ask, what about Calderón's War on Drugs and all the army Humvees and federal police trucks patrolling around?

"The day that the federal government launched Operation Culiacán-Navolato, Culiacán looked like a military parade," says Juan Carlos. "More than 1,500 soldiers and federal police officers rolled into town, and within an hour cartel assassins executed some guy in front of the Autonomous University of Sinaloa. That was when we knew that the Operation would be useless. The narcos assessed the efficacy of that operation instantly."

Earlier that day Pepis and I met for lunch to talk about journalism and violence in Culiacán. Pepis' 14-year-old son came with him. Pepis is a family man. He took his job folding the morning paper at *Noroesta* because his wife was pregnant with their first child and he wanted to get a job with a health plan. Now they have four children and Pepis works the night shift for *Primera Hora*. Even so he makes a point of driving home to eat dinner with his family every night. One night on such a drive he had just passed through a traffic light when a gun battle broke out.

"Sometimes I get sick of the life here," he told me over a lunch of *gorditas*, northern-style thick corn tortillas that are opened up and stuffed with beef, pork, chicken mole, chilies or beans and cheese. "Sooner or later my kids or someone in my family is going to get mixed up in this, be it directly or indirectly. If we live in a violent city, one day something will happen. There are many innocent victims here. I've thought of moving, but it becomes a lifestyle. It becomes a way of life, coexisting with crime and violence becomes a way of life. If they kill someone right here," and he points out to Culiacán's central plaza, "it won't cause a big stir, and this is a busy place. A bunch of people will crowd around the body and that's it. It doesn't shock that they've killed people right here in the city center, because they've committed so many high-impact atrocities worse than that."

After a few bites he looks over to his son and says, "A kid like him growing up in all this is thinking what he needs to do to get a new car, carry a good pistol, and go around town with a girl by his side. That's what the youth of today think. They live day to day. They're living only for the moment; they don't think about having a family, starting up some business, or studying.

"And the drug cartels here utilize this way of thinking to catch adolescents and use them as disposable triggermen. Why? A disposable triggerman won't cause you any headaches. You'll use him to kill ten or twenty people and when you know that he's not useful anymore, you yourself kill him. And the people say he's dead because he was up to no good. They use stolen new cars and give them a car and a pistol and a wad of cash. Ten years ago a hired gun would charge you an average of $1,500 to kill somebody, depending on the rank of the person to be killed. In some cases they'd charge almost $10,000, but the least they'd charge you would be $1,500. Do you want to know how much they charge now, or rather how much they pay them? They pay them about

$300 a week. They give them weekly salaries. How much can these kids save up in the short lives they lead? How much can they save? Not even enough to pay for a funeral."

"These are disposable assassins."

We arrive during the very last moments of dusk in the small rural town of La Palma, Navolato municipality. Within moments it is completely dark.

The body lies on the side of the road a few feet from a high white wall that stretches into the distance, enclosing a private property. Some twenty officers of the Culiacán state police force stand guard wearing bulletproof vests and holding machine guns at the ready. Some wear black masks covering their heads and faces. There are no Navolato municipal police present. Two police trucks are parked a few feet away, one on either side of the body, and their headlights illuminate the scene. A state forensics team gets to work, noting the position of the body and the bullet casings. The same man from Emaus that I saw an hour or so ago paces back and forth, talking on his mobile phone. Pepis gets to work.

This is not just any street, but the main highway that cuts through town. There are about a hundred residents crowded across the street, watching the scene. Some push forward into the street as far as the police will let them, about twelve or fifteen feet away from the body. Men and women, young and old, all press together, watching. Some twenty adolescent boys and young men on the edge of the crowd stand over their bicycles. Girls and boys, small children and babies in their parents' arms, also take in the spectacle. Families. Most watch in silence, some make hushed comments amongst companions; some of the teenagers and young men crack jokes and laugh.

The man's body—no one knows his name—lies on its back. His arms have been placed over his abdomen, crossed. On the wall behind him you can see bullet holes and splattered blood over the white paint.

Pepis walks from one side to the other, around the periphery established by the state police. They do not use caution tape, but rather stand in the road with rifles poised, a presence that clearly marks a first perimeter for the crowd. A smaller group of police forms a second perimeter closer to the body, this one meant for the photographers. I walk through the first perimeter it as if I had a right to and the police eye me, but then say nothing when they see me speak to Marco. Pepis crouches down and clicks his shutter. Standing several yards away still, the body lies mostly in shadow. Something seems amiss about the shape of the body, but I don't stare too long.

The crowd observes and comments, the police scan the crowd, shift their weight from one foot to the other. The forensics team goes through the motions of registering the central facts of the crime scene: body placement, locations of bullet casings, and distances between the two. I scrawl observations in my notebook.

And then gunfire rings out. Close. Loud. A machine-gun burst of some seven or eight shots. Quick and to the point. The entire crowd—spectators, police, reporters, everyone—lurches and then stills. Everyone looks around, scanning all sides. No one is coming. The shots came from the other side of the white wall not more than a hundred yards away. Once it seems that an armed convoy of professional killers is not careening toward us, the young men with their bicycles start to make jokes, "Here come the men with the masks!" And they laugh. But the families, the men, women, and children, start to move away. With unhurried but decisive steps, they head to their homes. Within mere moments the twenty or so boys and young men are the only spectators left. One of them says, "They left us all alone."

The police, detectives, and forensics inspectors also make a move. One detective says, "Let's go, pick him up already." And with that the forensics team, a few police, and the man from Emaus lift the body onto a stretcher, take it to the forensics van, and drive off. The police pile into two trucks and follow. The crime scene investigation is done.

Total time between hearing the machine-gun fire and the exit of a hundred onlookers, twenty police, and another twenty or so inspectors, funeral parlor employees, and reporters: Five minutes.

Notice that none of the twenty heavily armed and armored state police officers thought to investigate who had fired a machine gun nearby, itself a federal crime. On the contrary, the response was *Hurry up and let's go*. And of course it was. For the state police response perfectly illustrates a central fact of the drug war; the trade's death squads are more heavily armed and better trained than the on-duty state and local police, and most often the police are on their payroll anyway.

The machine-gun burst was a message that the residents and police understood unequivocally: Enough theater. We still have work to do. Move on.

As we get in the truck and leave, we see an army Humvee, with a soldier gripping a mounted .50-caliber machine gun on top, pull up on the corner and park, right across the street from the wall where the man was executed and beyond which someone had fired a machine gun a few minutes before. Clueless soldiers on patrol? Or fodder for those who say that the army supports El Chapo? Impossible to say, though it did seem a striking coincidence. How could the soldiers just happen to be right around the corner and yet not hear the shots or not care to investigate who might have committed the federal crimes of possessing and firing an illegal assault rifle?

I glance back. The street is deserted, the blood still wet on the wall, the Humvee calmly parked on the side of the road.

On the drive back I ask the *Primera Hora* team why they think the blood news, *la nota roja* is so popular in Mexico. Marco says, "The *nota roja* becomes a thing to do, like going to the movies. You're not sitting in a movie theater; instead you're at the scene of a crime. You saw how that little girl ran up barefoot, looking all around, smiled at me and then in a hurry looked at the dead guy. So, think of it like having the cinema on a personal level."

I did see the girl, about seven or eight years old, wide-eyed and smiling. She hurried up to get a close peek and then ran back to her family. Death as entertainment.

Back at the bunker everyone gets to work. I pull up a chair behind Pepis to watch him scan through his photos and select images to send to his editors. The photographs are much more intense visually than the experience of being there standing across the street and watching. The camera takes you closer than the police will let you go.

In countries like the United States and Japan—with globally dominant economies—there are industries capable of producing multimillion-dollar spectacles of fictional death for mass consumption. Such spectacles of death come in numerous varieties and subgenres. Westerns, action, suspense, gangster, and martial arts films all mostly involve death, if not gore. War and horror films of course are typically orgies of blood, death, and bodily destruction. For the price of approximately two hours' work at minimum wage, people in the United States can sit back and gawk for 90 to 120 minutes—munching on popcorn and sipping soda all the while. In Mexico, for the price of an hour's work at minimum wage, people can pick up the daily rag and gawk all they like. In the United States the price of admission also includes the luxury of knowing that the death you enjoy on the screen is fiction. The Mexican blood news includes no such luxury.

And it is only now, looking at Pepis's photographs, that I see the level of destruction unleashed upon whoever that body in Navolato belonged to. He was not only killed, he was destroyed. Pepis flips through the images and says, "I like this shot; it has good light." He is right; it does have good light. Pepis had turned off his flash and used the police headlights to illuminate the body while crouching down and shooting the picture from an angle. The image shows what the bullets did to that man's head and face. No tricks, no darkroom or Photoshop manipulation; the image does not lie. I was there, but I did not see it like this. The image is so grotesque that even the *nota roja* editors will decline to use it.

Pepis looks at me and asks, "What do you think, John?" He is not asking about the quality of the photograph. We both stare at the image—one of the most revolting I've ever seen—in sharp resolution on his computer screen. His voice is slow and heavy as it carries this question, which is not meant to provoke or mock. It is a deeply sad question.

"IT IS NOT NECESSARY for someone to show up and threaten you," said Javier Valdez Cárdenas, reporter and cofounder of the Culiacán-based weekly *Ríodoce*. "This situation is already a threat. It is as if someone were pointing a gun at you at every moment. The narcos control many parts of the country; they control governments and they control the newsroom. When you write an article about the narcos you don't think about your editor. You don't think about the news director. You don't think about the reader. You think about the narcos and whether they'll like it, whether they'll have a problem with it, whether they'll be waiting outside to take you away. The narcos control the newsroom."

Ríodoce, which means River Twelve (there are eleven rivers in the state of Sinaloa), is an independent weekly newspaper founded by four veteran Sinaloan journalists in 2003. They left their jobs at Culiacán's main daily, *Noroeste*, started *Ríodoce* from scratch, reported for years without a salary, went into the streets to give away issues, went door-to-door, and personally convinced newspaper stands and convenience stores to stock their paper, and now *Ríodoce* is read by more than six thousand people across Sinaloa, and followed by many more online. Every week the paper sells about 97 percent of its print run. A few years ago the U.S. Embassy in Mexico City—with a large DEA outpost—ordered a subscription to *Ríodoce* and purchased a copy of their entire archive of back issues. Pepis described them this way, "The *Ríodoce* reporters are the only *faquires* covering narco." In Spanish a *faquir* is a circus performer who swallows swords, fire, and poisonous animals without getting hurt.

Javier Valdez was born and raised in Culiacán and has worked as a journalist here for more than twenty years. He has written several books, including *Miss Narco* (2009) and *Malayerba* (2010), both of which chronicle the drug war in Sinaloa. Not only does he manage to cover the drug war and stay alive, he somehow maintains a zany, raunchy sense of humor. While we spoke at a café one day he received a call on his cell, politely said, "Excuse me, I have a call," and answered. Someone on the other line told him that three police officers had just been killed in nearby Elota. He hung up and called an official at the Sinaloa state attorney general's office and said, "*Culito, te extraño*"—which roughly translates as, addressing a man, "Little buns, I miss you"—and then without skipping a beat asked, "Yo homes, what do you know about three police getting killed in Elota?" He grabbed a napkin and took notes, thanked the official, and then hung up and said to me, "Confirmed."

Ríodoce is a necessary first stop for anyone arriving in Sinaloa with the task of trying to understand something about the drug business, drug politics, drug culture, and daily life in the state the majority of Mexico's most wanted *capos* call home. So many, in fact, come knocking on their door that the paper's staff members have a word for those foreign reporters—and by foreign they mean from anywhere beyond the borders of the state of Sinaloa—who call them up asking for information, contacts, leads, tips, and rides and then disappear without a trace. They call them *saqueadores*, or plunderers.

"There are people who come to squeeze information out of us," said Valdez. "What we try to do is take care of them, orient them well. But they never ask about you as a person. They never ask about your family. They could care less. What they want is for us to give them facts, contacts, information, photographs, and even very sensitive information. We call these people plunderers. They are vampires. They come, suck us dry, and they go away. We don't hear anything from them again until the next time they need something. These people didn't even care how we were doing after somebody threw a grenade at our office last September [2009].

"The plunderers don't just take information, but they

don't even cite us as the source. They use us and they expose us to danger too. For example, I take them in my car and I tell them, 'Hey, if we're going to such-and-such a place we need to be quick, like a boxer, get in and get out, like my dad use to say.' And sometimes they don't respect this. And they leave and I stay here. My car has license plates, it is not bulletproof, and the license plates are registered in my name. And then they are so stupid that they'll call us up and ask questions over the phone, very heavy questions. And even if you don't answer them, even if you hang up then and there, you're screwed because you know people are listening in and perhaps thinking, 'And why would they ask this guy that question?' We don't need to keep putting up with people like that. They need to go fuck themselves, speaking in scientific terms."

I spoke with Javier Valdez without any ambitions of plunder. I did not want to steal their scoops, mine their contacts, or ask them to drive me out to see marijuana and poppy fields. Instead I had three questions in mind. First, how can one do a good job reporting on the drug beat?

"No one is doing a good job of reporting the drug world, I'm certain of that," Valdez said. "There is no way to tell the story of everything that is happening here. So what we do is tell a part of it, what we hope is an important part. How do we do that? We have a lot of information. And I'm not talking about tall tales and secondhand gossip but solid, confirmed, firsthand information from high levels. And so what we have to do is administer that information and thus administer the risk. There are narcos that travel around with twenty gunmen everywhere they go. You can't risk yourself with that kind of impunity. You don't want them to point all those guns at you. The government should protect you, but it doesn't. And so we have the macabre play between the real and the possible. And it is always frustrating, because we have a lot of information that is waiting, holding on for other times."

Valdez writes breaking news, investigative articles, and a weekly column called *Malayerba*. In his news and feature pieces it is a constant balancing act, as he said, between "the real and the possible" but still manages to break national stories about the inner dynamics of the major cartels. In early 2009 he broke the story of a narco pact and its subsequent breaking two months later.

In *Malayerba* he profiles the daily stories of the drug world, stripping them bare of names, precise locations, and dates so as to leave everything just abstract enough not to incur, he hopes, the wrath of those implicated. The result is a literary treatment of the drug world composed entirely of facts based on reporting and firsthand, obviously anonymous, sources.

Another question I wanted to ask Valdez was this: how did this war begin?

"For a long time the fighting was just between them," Valdez said. "In the seventies, in the eighties. Everyone said, 'The narcos live in Tierra Blanca' [a neighborhood in Culiacán]. They didn't kill innocent people. Back then they still said not to kill women or children. I interviewed a paid killer one time who told me that he suspended the execution of a police chief once because the chief was with his mother. He killed him later."

In the time of Amado Carrillo Fuentes in the 1990s, he said, it was a different type of organization. They understood each other. They saw each other face to face; they had regular meetings. When Amado Carrillo died in 1997 the Sinaloa-based organization split into two rival factions, one supporting the leadership of Amado's brother Rodolfo, and another supporting El Chapo. Then, a few years later, and in the midst of this war, Chapo's organization split with the Beltrán Leyva brothers.

"It is a domestic fight," Javier said. "They were business partners, friends, godparents to each other's children, family. The people from the different groups knew each other, worked together, and some were lovers. They knew each other personally, intimately. Hence the scale of the feud, and why I say it is a domestic fight, a fight in the home. From one bedroom they shoot into another. Some seek refuge in the bathroom and others in the kitchen. And that got extended throughout the entire country. And the government let it happen. The Beltrán Leyvas formed an alliance with Chapo's enemies, and that extended the war to other regions of the country and made it crueler. I'm convinced that the Sinaloa Cartel has been less attacked, that it has been privileged. They do it because the Sinaloa Cartel doesn't use extortion, makes less noise, and is less bloody."

A third question: what can be done?

"I am an activist of pessimism," Valdez said. "The fire is going to spread. And the worst of it is not only the dead, but also the lifestyle that narco imposes on us all. I am speaking of the fear. We have already ceded the public parks and the park benches to the narcos, to fear. And I think that is the worst loss. This society is ill. There is no place for optimism in this scenario. And I say this with a great deal of sadness. I have children. And I tell them that there are other ways of life, other countries.

"How can you change all this? Well, by enforcing the law, the rule of law. I don't think there is any drug war. All they do is respond to violence with violence. A real drug war would spend resources on education and health and combating poverty. That would be a war against drugs, because it would take away the narco's most fertile terrain, youth."

At the end of the conversation I asked Javier Valdez, "Taking into consideration that it is impossible to cover the drug war well as a reporter, still what advice would you give to those coming here to give it a try?"

"Don't come here and count the dead," he said. "Anyone can do that. Tell the stories of life. Profile the fear, which is another death that no one covers; it is an encroaching death, and it is the worst."

I went to *Ríodoce*'s offices to speak with Ismael Bojórquez, the paper's director and main editor, who continues to report and write as well. If Javier Valdez is the poet-storyteller of the drug beat, Ismael Bojórquez is the senior analyst. When I told Diego Osorno, the Mexico City-based reporter and author of the book *El Cartel de Sinaloa*, that I had interviewed Bojórquez at length, Diego nodded gravely and said, "He is one of the people who knows the most about narco in this country."

Ríodoce rents a small office space with four rooms on the second floor of a nondescript two-story, concrete building in central Culiacán, above a print shop. The inside is spare: two desktop computers, three simple wooden desks, a small conference table, and a bookshelf.

Ismael Bojórquez's desk holds a laptop and a stack of documents, newspapers, and magazines. I began with the same question I asked Valdez, phrased a bit differently: How can one cover the drug war well?

"The thing is you can't cover it well. We've understood that pretty much since we started this newspaper," Bojórquez said. "We realized that we couldn't cover it well, and it makes sense: the narcos will screw you, the narcos will kill you. You can write about politics, but narco is another thing altogether.

"There are lines you can't cross. For example, the narcos don't like you to get involved with their families. You can't say that narco so-and-so lives in that house; they'll kill you the following day. You can't say that they own ranches or that one just bought such-and-such a shopping center. We don't just take a lot of precaution with this issue, but a *shitload* of precaution. There is absolutely no protection from the state for those who work as journalists. They can't even protect themselves, much less us.

"There are no clear rules in this shit. You develop a nose for it as you go along. There are lines, but they are very thin. What we have got clear is that you can't do your job in such a way that it could be confused at some point with a police officer's job. Your work has to be that of a journalist. If the narcos clearly see that your work is journalistic and not in anyway confused with what the police do, that might help you somewhere down the line."

Two days later I went back to *Ríodoce* to speak again with Ismael Bojórquez. I asked him, "How would you define this war?"

"I don't think it is a war," he said. "It is *Calderón's war*; it is his war. It is not a traditional war, there aren't two armies confronting each other. It is a biased war waged by Calderón. It is a bellicose struggle of shoot-outs and raids. But it is a totally incomplete struggle. Since it started we've seen that it is a war with too much circus. They called the journalists and took them off to a village in the mountains where all of a sudden planes flew overhead ejecting paratroopers. A lot of show, few results.

"Calderón did not attack the *narcopolítica* [politicians collaborating with drug mafias]; he never attacked them. There is another aspect that Calderón has never attacked, and this is much more serious; he never went against the financial and economic structure of the drug mafias. There has not been any intelligence work done on the financial channels of the narcos. So, as I say, there are two things Calderón never attacked: the economy of the drug mafias and their political connections.

"We live here. We're from Sinaloa. We know how the iguana chews its food. We know how drug money moves here. In fact, we know which businesses the drug mafias own, and there are many more we don't know about. And we know which politicians are in on this shit, too. And so you have to ask yourself, Well, if there is a war against drug trafficking, why doesn't Calderón combat all this? Why doesn't he investigate those people? And why doesn't he investigate these businesses?"

There is one case, mentioned briefly above, where some might be tempted to argue that Calderón's administration did in fact go after what Bojórquez calls the *narco-política*. One should avoid the temptation. Consider this, on May 26, 2009, federal police and soldiers detained ten mayors, seventeen officials ranging from the governor's aides to police officers, and also one judge in the state of Michoacán. In the following days they detained another mayor and six more officials, for a total of thirty-five arrested officials, an unprecedented sting operation in Mexico's drug war. The television cameras were on the scene to capture the images of disgraced mayors and cops leaving their offices with their jackets pulled up over their faces, escorted by heavily armed, masked soldiers and federal police. Reports of the arrests dominated the nighttime news broadcasts and the next day's headlines. The federal Attorney General's office accused them all of participating in organized crime. All of those arrested were members of the opposition PRD party. The PRD controls the state government and most municipalities in Calderón's home state of Michoacán. The arrests took place six weeks before the 2009 federal midterm elections in Mexico. A year and a half later, by late September 2010, thirty-four of the thirty-five Michoacán officials and police arrested back in May 2009 had been released for lack of evidence. The one mayor still being held had not yet been convicted of any crime. The national daily *Milenio* ran this front-page headline on September 29, 2010, "The Michoacán sting operation ended in ridicule" ("*Acabó en ridículo el michoacanazo*"). The story began thus: "The Attorney General's office appeared ridiculous [yesterday when] the most important investigation of this presidential term, the *michoacanazo*, came tumbling down."

Bojórquez's point stands. By fall of 2010 Calderón's billion-dollar drug war had resulted in no high-level politicians or money launderers being arrested, no major businesses or banks closed down, no large accounts frozen. The army killed people daily, but no serious combat against the drug mafias' political or economic structures had been waged.

And what can be done?

"The mafia is not going to disappear," Bojórquez said. "Drug trafficking is not going to disappear. But the intelligent objective I think would be to reduce it to a more or less tolerable level. Reducing the levels of violence, but also reducing the levels of contamination in the state. Now the state is totally contaminated by the drug mafias. All the institutions of the damn state, even the departments of social development that support the narcos through livestock programs, agricultural equipment, subsidies, fertilizers and through the treasury, through the communications departments that give them flight permits for their small planes. Everything is contaminated, man, and that's not to mention the army."

I asked if when he said "reduce it to a tolerable level" he meant negotiate.

"I'm not talking about negotiating," he said. "I don't think that the government should negotiate with the narcos; I don't believe in that strategy. In the short term it might solve problems with the violence, but I see it as an illusion. I think negotiations with the drug mafias will give them oxygen, will give them more strength to grow larger. I say such strategies should be discarded. I think that is what the government is doing and that it is going about it all wrong. I think the government is negotiating with a fraction of the drug traffickers, those from Sinaloa. But I think it is mistaken and that in the end it will not bring peace, because the organizations they are fighting like the Gulf Cartel, Carrillo Fuentes, Beltrán Leyva, are too big, too strong. They won't eliminate them. They won't bring peace to the country; on the contrary, they are letting the Sinaloa Cartel do their business.

"The government is making a mistake in that I think

they are making agreements with the Sinaloa Cartel. And that is because we see signals, like how El Chapo goes off to conquer Juárez and receives support there. So I think the government's strategy is to ally itself with the Sinaloa Cartel to strike against the Zetas, the Gulf Cartel, the Carrillos, and the Beltráns. And the government is doing this not only by providing protection through the army, but in joint operations. Indeed, I can confirm that there have been joint operations in the sense that soldiers and police officers together with cartel gunmen carry out some operations against the other cartels; we have detected that here. I think the government is wrong in this strategy because they work from the idea that the Sinaloans are pure narcos, that they are narcos that only traffic in drugs without getting involved in the other areas like extortion, charging protection money, and so on. And I think they are mistaken, because they are giving greater strength to what is perhaps the strongest drug-trafficking group in Mexico, the Sinaloa Cartel."

IT IS SIX O'CLOCK in the morning on August 31, 2009, when Salomón Monárrez hears the first shot. Sinaloa is a hot place to be in late August, and a shirtless Salomón Monárrez had opened the front door of his house to let in the morning breeze and walked back inside when the shot rang out. He turns back to the doorway, feeling the burn in his ear and drops of blood falling over his collarbone. He faces his killer, a dark, thick man of average height wearing camouflage pants, a black baseball cap, and black sunglasses.

Salomón Monárrez looks from the gun barrel to his killer's dark glasses and thinks, "Coward."

The killer grips the pistol in both of his hands, chest high, and walks forward as he fires. Salomón Monárrez jumps back and to the side, back and to the other side, like a football player evading tackle. With each step a bullet catches him in midair and throws him back—one in his left arm, one in his right arm, and then two in his left side. He repeats this three times and each time is hit in the air until a bullet slams into his abdomen and knocks him straight to the ground. Four more shots ring out, but somehow none of them hit. His killer stands over him. Salomón Monárrez looks at him and thinks, "What a coward you are. How can you come attack someone defenseless, someone without so much as a nail clipper in hand, and you with a pistol? What a coward." This he thinks with rage as he waits for the bullet that will enter his head and end his fifty-nine years of life. His killer pulls the trigger and no shot fires. The killer's gun jams; he looks down at Salomón Monárrez already drenched in blood, turns, and walks away.

Salomón Monárrez has six bullet wounds in his body. He thinks, "By nightfall I will be mourned." His arms burn. His left ear feels like someone has just extinguished a cigarette against it. His stomach burns. He takes this inventory of burning without moving, without trying to sit or stand. He lifts his head just a bit and sees his body covered in blood and feels life slip from him, as if someone were unplugging his life and then plugging it back in. His vision pulses from blurred to clear in time with this slipping of life. He moves his feet to see if they still work and they do. He cannot see his legs. "How many bullets hit my legs?" he thinks. But not one had. He breathes and thinks, "Let's see if I can fight. Let's see if they can save my life, if the doctors can save my life." An ambulance arrives. The paramedics rush Salomón Monárrez to the hospital.

Soon after army soldiers arrive at his house—before the municipal homicide detectives and state forensics team—pick up all the bullet casings, move things around, and leave.

In the ambulance Salomón Monárrez does not lose consciousness, but keeps feeling this unplugging and plugging back in of his life. At the hospital he feels the needle pierce his skin to administer the anesthetic and he thinks, "I won't be coming back. I'll be one more in the body count."

But no, six hours later, around noon, Salomón Monárrez comes back.

I met Salomón Monárrez nearly a year after he took six bullets and lived. He was sitting in the offices of the Frente Cívico Sinaloense (Sinaloa Civic Front), a Culiacán-based human rights organization that he and several colleagues founded in 1993. I dropped by one afternoon and introduced myself as a journalist from the United States. The first thing Monárrez asked me was "What impression do people there have of us here with all this death?" As I fumbled to avoid the most truthful response—most people in the United States do not even notice and many do not care—he continued:

"Last year they tried to kill me. They shot me six times and I had to leave Sinaloa. It is an ugly feeling to see death up close like that. After someone tries to kill you everything changes, everything. One is left practically disabled. This arm doesn't really work anymore. They shot me in the abdomen. It is a miracle that I'm here talking to you. They left me for dead.

"The hit on me was undoubtedly for our work here," he went on, "because we have been very strong, very harsh in documenting atrocities, assassinations, and kidnappings. We have been relentless."

What did Salomón Monárrez do to attract the attention of a professional killer? He did not mention local drug traffickers or gunmen by name. He did not publish information about properties owned by drug lords. He did not investigate drug money in local political campaigns. What brought an assassin to his doorstep was different. He and his colleagues at the Sinaloa Civic Front demanded justice in the cases of two massacres committed by soldiers of the Mexican army. They took a lawsuit to the Supreme Court arguing that military personnel who commit crimes against civilians should be judged in civilian courts. That is not a popular idea with the top brass in the military.

On June 1, 2007, a little before 9:00 p.m., some twenty soldiers opened fire on a pickup truck approaching a roadblock on a narrow, unpaved mountain road in Sinaloa, near the small community of La Joya de los Martínez in the municipality of Badiraguato, Sinaloa. The eight people packed into the pickup truck were on their way back from a day trip to Ocorahui, some fifteen miles away. Once a month, rural teachers in the region travel to Ocorahui for continuation courses and to collect their salary of about $120.

Three young teachers—Griselda Galavíz Barraza, 24, Alicia Esparza Parra, 19, and Teresa de Jesús Flores Sánchez, 19—were in the truck. Griselda Galavíz Barraza's husband, also Alicia Esparza Parra's brother, Adán Abel Esparza Parra, 29, was driving. Their three children were with them: Juana Diosminey, 2, Grisel Adonai, 4, and Edwin Leonel Esparza Galaviz, 7. Their nephew Josué Duvah Carrillo Esparza, 5, was also with them. Adán Abel Esparza Parra had taken his children, and their cousin Josué Duvah, to visit their grand-parents in Ocorahui while the three women were in class.

The truck came slowly around a bend—it is impossible to drive very fast on those roads—and was met with gun-fire before they could even see who was shooting at them. Bullets pierced the windshield. Adán Esparza was shot in the hand. He stopped, got out of the truck, and stood with his arms in the air shouting out, "Stop shooting! My family is in the truck!" The soldiers opened fire again, shooting Esparza's other hand and knocking him to the ground. At that point the truck began slipping backward, toward the edge of the road and the edge of a steep cliff. Esparza ran back to the truck to try and stop it, but his hands, destroyed by gunfire, would not respond to his commands. The truck fell back and over the cliff, rolling until stopped by trees. But Esparza's sister, wife and three children had already been killed by gunfire. His nephew Josué Duvah and Teresa de Jesús Flores Sánchez were wounded but survived.

The army roadblock was there to detect and detain drug traffickers. Seven of the soldiers who massacred Adán Esparza's entire family tested positive for marijuana, and one of the seven also tested positive for cocaine.

On the night of March 26, 2008, ten men were traveling in a Ford Lobo and a Hummer H2 in the municipality of Badiraguato, near the community of Santiago de los Caballeros. They were on their way home from a barbecue. The four men in the Lobo noticed that they no longer could see the Hummer's headlights behind them. After a few minutes they stopped to wait. After another few minutes they turned back. About half a mile down the road an army convoy stopped them and would not let them through.

The white Hummer H2 had over seventy bullet holes in the roof, side doors, and front windshield. Soldiers had fired upon the vehicle from an ambush position in the hillside on either side of the road. Six men were traveling in the vehicle; five died. There were no drugs or guns in the vehicle. When the soldiers approached the Hummer and realized that the men were unarmed they began to fight amongst themselves: "What did you do?" "Who shot first?" "Idiots, what did you do?" Wilfredo Madrid Medina, 22, was still alive. Only one bullet had grazed his head. When the soldiers realized he was alive they cursed him and began to beat, punch, and kick him and took him off to an empty nearby clinic. He thought they were going to kill him. Local residents soon crowded around, saving his life. After six hours an ambulance took him to the hospital, but federal officials then took him out of the hospital and detained him for questioning.

The next day the army sent out a press release that read, "On the 26th of the current month an incident took place near the community of Santiago de los Caballeros, municipality of Badiraguato, Sinaloa, in which two soldiers and four civilians lost their lives and two soldiers and one civilian were injured; one civilian was detained and turned over to an agent of the Federal Public Prosecutor." The army lied. The press release conflated two separate incidents that took place in different places and at different times to make it look as if the massacred family had been involved in a shoot-out and had killed two soldiers. As Javier Valdez reported in *Ríodoce* on March 31, 2008, two soldiers were indeed killed and one wounded, but on the other side of Badiraguato municipality, near San José del Llano.

By May 2008, during the first year and a half of Felipe Calderón's drug war, the Mexican National Human Rights Commission received 634 complaints against the army for abuses ranging from murder to torture to robbery. (One year later the number of complaints would rise to more than two thousand.) The human rights activists at the Sinaloa Civic Front faced the escalation of army abuses and thought, what would happen if soldiers could be tried in civilian courts for crimes against civilians? They worked with the Mexico City-based Miguel Agustín Pro Juárez Human Rights Organization to take the cases of army massacres

of civilians to the Supreme Court as justification to re-
voke special military jurisdiction for crimes soldiers commit against civilians.

On July 27, 2009, *Ríodoce* published a front-page article
about the Supreme Court case. A full-color photograph of
soldiers, armed and standing at attention, appeared under a
headline that read, "Army on the sidelines: Court to review
military jurisdiction for Santiago de los Caballeros massacre." One month later, at 6:00 a.m., Salomón Monárrez
looked past the barrel of a 9mm pistol and watched a man in
sunglasses shoot him to the ground.

Salomón Monárrez was not the first member of the
Sinaloa Civic Front to receive a bullet. On September 6,
2007, Ricardo Murillo Monge, who cofounded the organization together with his sister Mercedes and Monárrez,
was found in his car, parked near a gas station and a major
shopping mall in Culiacán, shot through the head. The day
before, a few men had come by the office looking for him.
They saw him from a distance and left. At the time Ricardo
Murillo, 66, was selling his car; it had a FOR SALE sign in
the window. The next day the men came back and asked
Ricardo Murillo to show them the car. He left with them,
leaving the light and air-conditioning on at his office. He
was next seen dead. The gas station near where he was left
has a closed-circuit video camera mounted on a wall. The
camera clearly captured the killers walking away from the
parked car. One of the killers even turned back and faced the
camera, apparently unaware he was being videotaped. The

camera stills, clearly identifying the killers, are in Ricardo Murillo's case file. Police never identified or detained these men, nor have they made an arrest in the case. At the time of his death, Ricardo Murillo was investigating the massacre of Adán Esparza's family near La Joya de los Martínez four months prior. A week before his murder he had held a press conference about the case. The day before his murder Ricardo Murillo decried the impunity of the army massacre of Adán Esparza's family on a radio show.

Mercedes Murillo, Ricardo's sister and the 74-year-old current president of the Sinaloa Civic Front, joined us in the office. Again I introduced myself as a journalist, and Murillo, also known as Meché, said, "Okay," took a seat, and proceeded to unleash the following appraisal of the situation.

"The only thing organized, well-organized, in Mexico is organized crime," she fired off. "Everything else is unorganized. How is it possible that in Mexico the government jumps off to a war where all the generals are divided? The PGR can't stand the SIEDO [the Assistant Attorney General for Specialized Investigations and Organized Crime], and neither of those two can stand the AFI [Federal Investigative Agency]. The army doesn't like the AFI, the SIEDO, or the PGR. And all these federal agencies can't stand the state agencies. So, what is happening in this war? Twenty-eight thousand people are dead.

"People have lost all faith in the authorities, the only thing in this war that we can believe in is the dead. So far in this six-year term [of Felipe Calderón's administration that began in December 2006] 3,000 people have been slain in Sinaloa. Today we read in the newspaper that 300 more federal police are coming to Sinaloa. And the question is: why? If thousands of soldiers came and the executions continued, and the violence continued. . . . Today we are worse off than before.

"So the Sinaloan Civic Front together with the Miguel Agustin Pro, went to the Supreme Court to ask that when a soldier commits a crime of civil jurisdiction, the soldier be tried by civilian courts. Because the way things are now the military killed these four people [in Santiago de los Caballeros] and we do not know where the trial stands because they are trying them with military prosecutors and before military judges. So we do not know what is happening. Along with the Miguel Agustin Pro Juarez we took this complaint to the Supreme Court and the truth is they sent us packing; they said no. They told us that soldiers can kill civilians the military will judge them. They will not be judged by civilians.

"Today in the midst of such hopelessness they start to talk about legalizing marijuana. If they legalize it or if they don't legalize it, the marijuana is everywhere. And it is the least harmful. He works in construction," she said pointing to Monárrez who owns a small contracting business, "and he'll tell you that he knows construction workers who have smoked marijuana for years and it's no big deal. But Sinaloa became a place for the transit of other drugs, not marijuana, but synthetic drugs including cocaine and this is now a transit place en route to the United States. And so what we most lament in Sinaloa are our dead. What we most lament in Sinaloa is that the government should launch a war without prior investigation, launch a war with everyone divided, launch a war where we don't know who is responsible for all our dead."

I asked both Murillo and Monárrez about the investigation into Monárrez's attempted murder. What is happening in the case?

"We don't know," Meché answered in a tired voice. "Who are you going to demand justice from? The governor? The President of the Republic? The state police? The federal police? The army? Just look at all these I'm naming. The SIEDO? The AFI? The PGR? Who? Who? Who is responsible for all that is happening in Mexico? That is a question that you journalists have to ask. Who is owning up to all this? Because it's not just that they are killing; the widows are left with nothing. There are thousands of orphans. It is not just a murder attempt, but also all the consequences that come after: work, family, the disintegration of everything you have. Disintegration everywhere you look—economic, political, social. That is the situation with drug trafficking, and no one is responsible, and they say it is a war, but we don't know what it is."

And her brother's case?

"The photos are in the case file, but nobody is looking for those men. That's why it's called impunity," she said.

"There are 28,000 murders so far in this war that started when Calderón took office and only 5 percent have been investigated. And thus the people of Mexico are contributing the dead and Calderón is contributing the politics."

FROYLÁN ENCISO, A BRILLIANT YOUNG SINALOAN historian of the drug trade, told me that if I wanted to report on the drug war in Sinaloa I'd have to get drunk. "At their offices people will treat you a bit coldly," he said. "They'll talk around the matter at hand and leave only hints and clues in code, and if you don't know the codes you'll be lost. People here talk straight when they drink. If you want to really find out what's going on you'll have to leave your notebook behind and get drunk." He told me this after about eight bottles of Tecate Light, the local favorite.

Unplanned, I had a chance to test Froylán's theory. A friend and his wife sent me a message that they were going to the Guayabo cantina one Saturday night and invited me along.

The Guayabo is a simple place with a jubilant atmosphere—"the only cantina in Culiacán untouched by narco," according to Javier Valdez, a habitué of the place for many years. Patrons whistle, throw peanut shells and dirty beer-soaked napkins, treat each other to drinks, and greet and taunt in a nonstop nonlinear dynamic that drips of camaraderie without any undertones of hostility or danger.

Vendors sell peanuts, chewing gum, cigarettes, fried pork skin, pirated DVDs and CDs, including the latest *narco-*

corridos, and offer electric shocks for $5 a hit. (The money is apparently not justified by the sensation itself but by the deep belly laughs afforded to the congenial crowd witnessing a first timer's reaction to a significant electrical shock.)

A high-angled thatched roof, ceiling fans whirling to diminish the heat, waitresses with name tags. Zurdo, the headwaiter, wears a white waiter's coat, left over from some twenty years of donning an all-white uniform from shirt to shoes he first put on one day when warned that an impending state health inspection required such attire. Said inspectors never arrived, but Zurdo (Lefty) kept the all-white dress until just a few years ago, when he allowed himself black shoes and pants.

Many cantinas in Mexico still do not allow women inside. But not the Guayabo. Women are welcome there, and it shows, though the crowd is still mostly men in their 40s and 50s.

At one point a young man lingered in the doorway, watching, scanning the crowd. A Culiacán native with his back to the door made subtle gestures with his eyes to keep a watch on the guy. The man, in his early twenties, tall and thin, with close-cropped hair, and a slow, purposeful gaze that did not correspond to looking for a friend on a Saturday night among the older crowd of a cantina, watched, observed, and then stepped away. This is a city where armed convoys shoot people dead on major avenues and no one ever seems to be pursued or caught. This is a street where, only an hour or so before, someone walking along the sidewalk could glance by chance into an auto repair shop just in time to see a man lift an automatic rifle from a table.

My friend and his wife noticed a high-level Sinaloa state government security official and invited him over for my benefit, saying maybe he'd give me an interview. He joined us and was soon drumming on the table to the 1950s Spanish rock tunes played by a virtuoso band of 60- and 70-year-old musicians. The conversation turned to the subject of reforming the police, recently in the headlines due to Calderón's "National Security Dialogue" in Mexico City. "What good will a sweeping police reform do if the public investigators [*ministerios públicos*] are not also reformed?" the security official asked.

He then looked to me and, apparently for the benefit of an outsider not familiar with local customs, added, "Not that it really matters; no one here investigates anything."

I asked him if anyone had been executed that day in Sinaloa. "Oh sure, I think about seven people," he said. "The daily average is seven or eight."

A lawyer by trade with many years' experience in state government, I asked him what solutions he saw, what possible ways out of the current situation of violence. He did not hesitate a second. "None," he said. "There's no way out. It will go on and it will get worse."

The conversation at the table turned for a moment to Cuba. The security official had traveled there and commented on how beautiful it was and how safe he felt there, though, at the same time, how intensely socially controlled it seemed.

"In order to have a foreign visitor in your house you have to have a permit," he said. "No sooner will a foreigner arrive for lunch than someone will knock on your door and ask to see your permit for having a foreign visitor in your house."

The state security official paused and then said, "I'd rather have Cuba's problems than the violence here. I'd rather my son live in Cuba with all the deprivation they have there, than live here and fear for his life every day."

I asked the official if I could interview him in the coming days in his office. "Of course," he said, "on Monday," and gave me his mobile phone number. I called on Monday and a secretary answered and took my message. I tried calling back later in the afternoon. The official said that he'd had "many problems to deal with," and asked if I could come by his office at 11:00 a.m. the next day. I said sure.

Although a total of fourteen people were executed in Sinaloa that day, the main problem was the discovery of five dead bodies inside the state prison in Culiacán. Four were found in a trash dump, inside the prison grounds, with their throats slit. The fifth was found dead, apparently of an overdose, in his bed. The discovery brought the total number of homicides committed inside Sinaloa state prisons during the first eight months of 2010 to sixty: twenty-three in Culiacán and thirty-seven in Mazatlán. That is as many people as had been killed in Sinaloa state prisons during the five previous years, 2005–2009. Of the four men found with their throats slit, three had been arrested only days before after a shoot-out with the army. Soldiers confiscated nine SUVs that had been reported stolen, assault rifles, grenades and grenade launchers, more than one thousand clips, and a Barrett .50-caliber sniper rifle. The soldiers arrested the three men on illegal weapons charges on Friday; by Monday morning they were dead. The fourth man found dead with them had been in jail since December 2009 on sexual assault charges.

I went to the Sinaloa Department of Public Safety the next day at 11:00 a.m. After I waited nearly one hour and was interviewed myself by the Department's public relations staff, the official came in, greeted me warmly, and invited the PR director and me into his office. He asked how he could be of help. I said that I would like to interview him about the general state of public safety in Sinaloa. He asked if I could write down my questions so that they could work on them and get back to me. I replied that I would prefer to talk and would be willing to come back at any time more convenient for them. The official repeated his request that I leave written questions. I said, of course. "And don't think I'm taking you for a ride," he said as we stood up. "We are committed to speaking with you and will stick to that commitment, because we will." I said thank you and went back into the PR director's office to leave my questions, which I knew would never be answered, and they weren't. Froylán Enciso was right. The sober official had no interest in talking.

While leaving my questions however, I thought I would try my luck: "Would it be possible to interview someone inside the prison?"

The PR director called one of her staff into her office.

"What do you think about taking him to the prison tomorrow to see Beni?"

"Tomorrow's perfect," the staffer responded. "They'll be doing the burning of the past."

They then explained to me that there is a drug rehabilitation program inside the prison called ¡Tu Puedes! (You Can Do It!). It is run by a prisoner—Beni—and the inmates in the program volunteer to be locked in a room together for a month and taken twice a day into a sauna in the same small building as the dormitory. Absolutely no drugs, alcohol, or cigarettes are allowed in the room. Anyone caught with any kind of intoxicant is immediately expelled. The manner in which the PR staff stressed and re-stressed that *really* no drugs are able to get in that room revealed a certain tacit official recognition that drugs are easily available everywhere else in the prison *except* that room. The "burning of the past," they said, is a ceremony in which participants throw an article of their clothing into a fire before they step into the dorm room for the month-long detoxification, leaving their past behind them.

I knew I was walking into a PR trap, a rigorously controlled room in a completely lawless prison where four dead bodies had just been dumped in the trash, but I thought I would surely see something interesting.

The next day on the drive out to the prison, I asked the PR staff what the prison population was. About 2,600. "But there are prisoners who are still here years after their sentences have been completed," the state employee told me.

"They don't check their case files; their lawyers don't check their case files. And you can't expect us to be checking 2,600 case files."

My custodian accompanied me through security—I was asked to leave my identification and was cursorily frisked— and took me to meet the warden. The PR guy introduced me, "a reporter from California," and said I was there to learn about the rehab program You Can Do It!

The warden, Carlos Suárez Martínez, is the man who, in theory, would need to explain how four prisoners ended up dead in the trash dump. He would need to explain how the killers got the weapons they used to slit four men's throats. He would need, in theory, to explain how the killers got access to their victims, killed them, and then carried their bodies out to the trash without any guards noticing and without any of the camera surveillance equipment recording them. On the morning of August 19, 2010, Carlos Suárez Martínez was a man with a lot of explaining to do, and thus a man who was probably not looking forward to being introduced inside the prison to a foreign reporter.

The PR guy stressed several times that I was there for the "burning of the past" and You Can Do It! Carlos Suárez Martínez looked me up and down and before I could say a word said "You Can Do It! Let's go meet Beni!" He then charged ahead followed by two large guards armed with machine guns.

On the walk through the prison courtyards over to the rehab area the warden stopped several times to point out fruit trees to me: papaya, banana, and avocado growing on small patches of thick mud amidst the sprawl of concrete. The warden plunged onward and stopped again around the corner to point out a mango tree. "This year we had a shitload of mangos," he said with a big smile, "a whole shitload!"

We ran into Beni, and the warden introduced me to him and excused himself. He had to attend to other matters. While I was at the prison that day Sinaloa Governor Jesús Aguilar Padilla and the warden announced that they would be firing the prison's two highest-ranking guards Pablo Ursúa Vásquez, chief of guards, and Guadalupe Nevárez Silva, chief of security. Four bodies in the trash and two people fired.

Beni is a tall, imposing figure. His presence commands respect. He was also extremely affable and easygoing when we spoke, a congenial fellow who had managed to turn his life around in the most heinous of situations. He is 40 years old and has been in prison for the past seventeen years. He was born in the tiny ranch of Los Lobitos in Badiraguato; by the age of 16 he was a trafficker and gunman for the Sinaloa Cartel. By age 18 he commanded a unit of fifteen people. Once, in 1991, U.S. undercover informants posing as buyers in the United States tried to bust him on a deal. He shot his way out, killing one of the informants, and fled over the border. Due to political pressure from the United States, the Mexican army and police were looking for him and finally caught him in 1993 at a highway roadblock. When he arrived in prison, he said, he had been using drugs socially—sniffing cocaine at parties, but not frequently. Inside prison, however, he became a heavy addict and a brawler. "I got to a very intense, deteriorated state," he said. "I was a bully, and I was always in the punishment cells." Once he spent a three-year-and-two-month stretch in solitary confinement—where, of course, drugs were still readily available through the guards. When he came out, he wanted a change.

In 2000, the Sinaloa state prison started the rehab program You Can Do It! Beni voluntarily entered as part of the first group of inmates to try the method. After making it through the detoxification process he applied himself diligently to the tasks, exercise routines, and classes that comprise the second phase. He showed exemplary discipline and requested to stay in the program. Ten years later, and still a prisoner, he now directs it. He has earned obvious privileges. He wears stylish blue jeans, cowboy boots, a leather belt with a large metal belt buckle, and a freshly pressed white button-down shirt with the You Can Do It! logo stitched on the chest pocket. Those who make it through the detoxification phase can chose to stay in the program, living in an isolated area from the rest of the prison population. Little by little, those who stay with the program and comply with its strict rules earn privileges like Beni's and can get time knocked off their sentences. Though they will need to keep on top of their own case files.

We went out to the courtyard for the "burning of the past" ceremony. Thirty-nine men and four women stood in four rows facing a large wood pyre. The warden returned and made a quick speech. "We don't care about the past any-more," he said, "leave it all behind, start afresh, you can do it." Then, to my surprise, he said, "We are joined today by a reporter from Los Angeles who is writing down everything we do." I looked up from my notebook and saw forty-three faces staring at me, some hard, some hostile, some curious, some empty, and one smiling.

Beni gave the order and they took off their T-shirts re-vealing You Can Do It! T-shirts beneath. They walked up to the pyre and threw their old shirts in; the flames dipped and then rose.

"Look!" Beni shouted out. "See how it stays behind, the past. From today forward we are new. We will turn our backs on the past. *Half turn, hut!*"

Beni then marched them into the small room where the thirty-nine men would spend the next month. The four women would be taken to a separate facility. Inside the room Beni read out the rules and marching orders of the program, most emphatically: no drugs, no alcohol, no cigarettes, no fighting, and no stealing. Any infraction whatsoever—no explanations—earns immediate expulsion. As Beni went through the rules I scanned the inmates' faces. Most appeared to be between 18 and 25 years old; no one in the crowd could have been older than 30. Many of their faces looked hardened and worn; some looked childlike and fresh. Most looked at me with only mild curiosity, a few with open hostility, and one with that strange grin. When the time came for the inmates to say good-bye to family who had come for the ceremony and would not be able to visit for the next ten days, I noticed that the grinning man was alone, so I went up to him and said hello. The man, Gabriel, was smiling because the warden had incorrectly introduced me as a reporter from Los Angeles. Gabriel grew up in Los Angeles. We then spoke in English, in my hope that the state PR guy clinging to me like a shadow would not understand and would start talking to someone else, which he did.

Gabriel was born in Culiacán but moved to LA at age 12 when his parents migrated there for work. He spent seven years in prison in California, both LA County and Folsom. I asked him why and he said "transportation." I asked again and he replied, "I was taking a thirty-five-pound load of crystal across the border." He had made many such trips before getting busted, he said. When he finished his sentence in California he was deported. I asked him why he had volunteered for the rehab program. "I don't have the vice of cocaine, but I do have the vice of smoking cigarettes," he said, "so I thought I'd quit." I asked him if the prison was rough. He shrugged his shoulders: "If you walk around like a badass then it can get pretty rough." Like Folsom, I asked? "No!" he said with a widening of his eyes, "over there it is hard time."

Later that day I dropped by the offices of the Sinaloa Civic Front to see what Meché Murillo had to say about the recent killings in the prison and the drug rehabilitation program.

"Well sure, they're showing you the pretty stuff," she

said, "and what's more they don't let you walk around freely. Why would you want to see the You Can Do It! program? It's a bunch of lies. For every twenty young men who go through that program, either all of them will go back to drugs, or maybe one will be saved. The young men go into the You Can Do It! program with the hope that they will have their sentences cut, not to cure themselves of the disease, because drug addiction is a disease. But even so, if four or five of them get off of drugs a year that justifies the program. Also, for the time they are there they detoxify, and that is good, maybe it will stretch out their lives a little.

"The security that they have there in the prison," she continued, "is among the worst in the world. They have cameras everywhere, but the cameras do not work. There are cameras all over that prison. How is it possible that they can kill people, slit their throats, and no one notices? Today the newspapers are saying that two guards are responsible. How did the weapons get in there? How did the knives get in there? The penitentiary system in Mexico will be the last thing to be reformed, because that is where the poorest people are. So they show you something that has a 5 percent success rate."

Murillo and her colleagues at the Civic Front spent several years working on a program to stop torture in Mexico's prisons, she told me. She has been inside every state prison in Sinaloa and spoken at length with prison officials, guards, and inmates. She said that prison wardens always struggle to keep their jobs because it is such good business.

"This I can guarantee you," she said, "the drugs get in through the front door. They do not get in through tubes or over fences or anything like that. They enter through the door. Weapons enter through the door, whether knives or pistols, they enter through the door."

Sinaloa recently changed the names of the state prisons from "Centers for Social Re-adaptation" to "Centers for the Implementation of Prison Sentences." In Spanish, the word for implementation, in this case, is *ejecución*, which also means, of course, execution. Meché said that the name change is accurate.

"There is no death penalty in Mexico, but inside the prisons the death penalty does exist," she said. "It is an execution center, but execute as in murder, not execute as in fulfill."

IN THE BATTLE ZONES of the drug war, where the soldiers sent into the streets to "keep drugs from reaching your children" shoot kids dead, where the cruelest of hired killers is called The Barbie, where the police will tell you that they do not investigate murder cases because they are afraid, the ambulances will not take people with bullet wounds to the hospital for fear that the killers will return to finish their victims off en route, in a place where such incongruity is the norm, perhaps it should not come as a surprise to find, here, a rare sign of hope in the actions of a woman who says she has lost all of hers.

Alma Trinidad Herrera has every reason to give up.

She has every reason to go home, shut her windows, lock her door, and grieve. She knows that her quest is more than quixotic; she knows that it is, by every measure of reason, futile. She knows that the entire weight of a global war—the full momentum of a multibillion-dollar industry, the entire architecture of the state, every government office from the local homicide detective to the governor, from the senate to the president, every last one of them—is against her. She knows that her request is impossible, and still she demands it.

This is what hope looks like here: a woman who will not go home and accept impunity as just the way things are; a woman who two years after her son was killed in a daylight massacre of eleven people still goes every two weeks to City Hall to demand progress in her son's murder investigation. There is no such investigation, of course, and there never will be, and that is what makes Alma Trinidad a lonely foot soldier of hope in a hopeless, desperate war.

The emergency brake on her Ford EcoSport failed when she went to park in the hilly neighborhood of Cañadas in Culiacán, Sinaloa. A few days later, on July 10, 2008, Alma Trinidad was at her office with her two sons when she asked her then 28-year-old son César if he would take her car to the shop.

"Sure thing," he said. "Let me call Chuy."

Jesús Alfonso López Félix, or Chuy, was César's friend from school and also a trained mechanic. Chuy would of-

ten do side repair jobs for his classmates and teachers. César
and Chuy studied accounting together at the Autonomous
University of Sinaloa, or UAS, in Culiacán. César and his
16-year-old brother, Cristóbal, both worked in their mother's small accounting office. Alma Trinidad also received her
accounting degree from the UAS.

César called Chuy and told him that his mother had a
problem with the emergency brake.

"Okay," he said, "bring it over and I can fix it right now,
real quick."

"Mom, if you want I can take it over to Jesús," César
said to his mother. "The shop where he works is pretty close,
and it's an easy thing to fix. It should be fast."

"Okay, sounds good," Alma said.

"Hey, wait up," said Cristóbal, who had been listening,
"I'll go with you."

They left. It was approximately 10:50 a.m.

César had never been to the shop where Chuy worked;
when Chuy had helped him with car problems before, he
would get under the hood right there in the university parking
lot. After driving in circles for a few minutes he called Chuy
again on his mobile phone to ask for directions.

"Head to Río Meca Street," Chuy told him, "and it's
about a block after the gas station. When you get close, call
back and I'll come outside."

And so he did. A few minutes later César called back,
saw Chuy waving from down the street, drove up and then
pulled the car into the driveway and parked. The place was

a simple rectangular, concrete warehouse converted into the Mega 2000 mechanic shop, specializing in bodywork and paint jobs. Nine cars and trucks, including five federal police trucks, were parked inside. Several more were in the driveway and parked in front. Jesús lifted the car up with a jack. And went under to take a look.

At that point two professors from the accounting and business school at the UAS, José Alfonso Ochoa Casillas, 61, and José Alfonso Ochoa Quintero, 37, father and son, pulled up. César and Cristóbal went up to say hello and talk for a bit. The manager of the shop joined the conversation. After a bit Cristóbal noticed the federal police trucks in the back of the workshop. The trucks were riddled with bullets from a shoot-out months earlier in which eight federal officers were killed. César and Cristóbal went back to check out the trucks when they heard what seemed like bottle rockets. César spun around, worried that perhaps his mother's car had fallen on Chuy. Then he saw the men, about six of them, wearing bulletproof vests and carrying AK-47 and AR-15 assault rifles loaded with two drum magazines, *los huevos del toro* (bull's balls), walking toward the shop, firing.

"Hide!" César said to his brother. "There's a gunfight outside." It seemed to César at first that the gun battle was out in the street. As he ran farther into the back of the shop, in between the cars, he did not feel afraid and was collected enough to think about the best place to hide from stray bullets; beneath one of the trucks, with his body aligned with the axle, his head behind one of the tire's rims, most likely too thick for a bullet to penetrate. As he jumped over the hood of a car to get over to the truck, a bullet tore into his leg just beneath the knee.

He crawled under the truck and watched as pairs of military boots entered the body shop. Only one of the gunmen wore white tennis shoes. A loud voice shouted out, "Kill every last fucking one!"

With each burst of gunfire César thought, "I hope Cristóbal is hiding; I hope Cristóbal is hiding." With each agonizing yell, he thought, "That's not Cristóbal, please let that not be Cristóbal."

A man came running back into the shop; shots rang out and the man fell. But he was not dead. He was looking straight into César's eyes, César lying on the floor under the truck. Perhaps so as not to be tempted to speak or make a gesture, the man turned his head to face the other way. The gunman must have seen it for he immediately unleashed a burst of gunfire and killed him. The gunman then walked further back into the shop, standing only feet away from César. Shots were ringing out from every direction.

"I hope my mobile phone does not ring, please," thought César. From where he was lying, he could see almost up to the mouth of one gunman across the shop. The ones he could see all looked thin, white-skinned, and young. Then the gunman took out a new clip to load into his assault rifle. But he dropped it. "If this asshole bends down to pick it up," thought César, "I'm dead."

At that moment, the same voice that issued the order

to kill everyone shouted again, "All right, let's go! Everyone out!"

The gunman turned and started walking out, loading his rifle with another clip pulled from his vest.

"I saw that everyone was dead," César told me when we spoke two years after the massacre. "I didn't see my brother, and I thought that he might have been able to hide. I waited a bit before getting out from under the truck, just in case one of them had stayed behind, or who knows. When I got up I called my mom. I told her what had happened, that there had been a shooting and I couldn't see my brother. I went up to Jesús. He was still alive. He had a bullet wound in his head and his arm. His arm and stomach were completely destroyed. He was able to speak and he asked me about his little daughter, and then if I could fan his face or give him mouth-to-mouth respiration. And I couldn't do it, because I was dying of nausea from all I saw. His arm was torn off, left just hanging. I told him, 'I'm going to look for my brother.' I went back to the back to see if he was still alive. And I saw that his eyes were open. And I couldn't see any bullet wounds. I said to him, 'Get up man! Let's get out of here!' But he didn't react. I slapped his face and when I went to lift him his jaw came loose and blood began to run everywhere. When I knew he was dead I started screaming with rage. I went back to Jesús and with another person we tried to fan him with a piece of cardboard. I was talking with him when he also died."

Jesús died asking César to help talk care of his daughter. Jesús was 24.

Everyone at the Mega 2000 body shop, except César, was dead: the two professors, father and son; the manager; four employees; Cristóbal and Jesús. And not just dead, but their bodies mutilated with gunfire. Blood everywhere. Spent bullet casings, some 300 rounds, everywhere. The smell of gunfire and ripped-open intestines.

After a bit the municipal police arrived, then the federal police, and then the army and Red Cross ambulances. The Red Cross would not let César, with a bullet wound in his leg bleeding profusely, into the ambulance. It was too dangerous, they said. The victim of drug war violence who survives becomes a threat to anyone near him or her by the very fact of survival.

Down the street, the gunmen had fired upon state and local police officers that happened by as they were leaving the scene of the massacre. One officer was dead and another barely holding on. The army and federal police had secured the area with scores of heavily armed troops standing guard on every corner.

"I felt protected," César said even though the Red Cross wouldn't take him to the hospital, "because the army was there, because all the police were there. I thought they were protecting me. Hah! As soon as the police officer died they all left."

What makes Alma Trinidad different is that, in this realm of dizzying contradictions, she demands that public officials simply do what they say they are there to do—and indeed, as she is quick to remind everyone, what they get paid to do. What makes her strange is that she too steps into the terrain of contradiction usually reserved for those in positions of power within the state. The politicians and police seem to assume that the victims and the disempowered will somehow accustom themselves to accepting impunity *in fact* while still believing in the rule of law *in the abstract*. Alma Trinidad knows the officials will do nothing, and yet she constantly, publicly demands that they do.

Two years after the massacre, the police have not made a single arrest in the case. On the day of the killings, the police called the man whose name was registered as the owner of the Mega 2000 body shop in to the station to testify. The man's testimony consists of his name, address, and how he learned of the massacre. The man has since disappeared. Mega 2000 never opened again; the building remains abandoned. The officials now say that they "do not know" who really owned Mega 2000. And yet that same day, as news of the shooting was posted on local newspaper websites, anonymous commentators wrote that the shop belonged to Gonzalo Inzunza Inzunza, alias El Macho Prieto, a notorious hired gun in the employ of El Chapo Guzmán and the Sinaloa Cartel.

"Everyone knows who owned the body shop," Alma Trinidad said. "If you ask the ice cream man, 'Hey, who owns that car shop where they killed those nine people?' he'll tell you. The attorney general seems to be the only one who doesn't know. That's Culiacán. The supposed owner was just a name on paper. The real owner is another, a real heavy other. They say that the killers went to heat up his territory."

At first she pronounced the name in public protests and interviews with the press until someone suggested she omit that one detail. Now she says, "You can't say his name here. You can't name him."

And yet everyone knows. There is even a *narco-corrido* about Macho Prieto's proclaimed pain and suffering upon learning of the massacre and his commitment to vengeance. The song, *La mente en blanco* (*My Mind is Blank*) by Voz de Mando (Voice of Command), can be heard on YouTube. Here are a few key verses from the lyrics:

> *My mind is blank*
> *They have touched my blood*
> *I can barely hold back the tears*
> *The damage is irremediable.*
> [...]
>
> *How my blood boils*
> *It hurts what they did to me*
> *They will pay for their treason*
> *They will have to deal with this*
> *I am enraged*
> *Why did they provoke me*
> *I'm already in the ring*

They killed innocent people
Who were not involved
And for this they will pay.
[...]

I am ready for combat
I have the highest-quality weapons
More than 300 people
Are under my command
With anti-tank guns, bazookas,
Bulletproof vests and AK-47s
To fuck them up
There will be no peace
I am not a traitor.

I am Mayo's blood [Ismael "El Mayo" Zambada, a
     leader of the Sinaloa Cartel]
With the boy [El Mayo's son, Vicente] *I remain firm*
I hang in Culiacán
Where I was born
And where I'll die
I've got all my boys
And we're well armed
Do not forget this
I am Gonzalo
My code is The Eleven
I am Macho Prieto

The song makes clear that the attack was against Macho Prieto, though the gunmen also killed innocent people. But it is just a song. It is not an official government document in the case file of a homicide investigation. In said case file the name Gonzalo Inzunza Inzunza, El Macho Prieto, does not appear.

And yet Alma Trinidad wants to know why not. She wants to know why the homicide investigators cannot find the supposed owner of the Mega 2000, and why they aren't looking for the real owner. She wants to know why five federal police vehicles were being repaired at a body shop owned by a high-level Sinaloa Cartel hit man. She wants to know who took those federal police vehicles there for repair and who authorized that repair.

The investigators do not want to know these things. They want the federal anti-organized crime investigative unit, the SIEDO, to take the case off their hands and make it go away.

"Look Ma'am, the truth," the investigators told Alma Trinidad, "we'll tell you, we're scared to get involved on this one."

"Is that so?" she responded. "Well, kid, if you're scared, what are you doing here? Why don't you go look for another profession that doesn't scare you? Leave this to someone who has the courage to actually do the work. Because if you're just sitting here acting stupid so they'll pay you. . . ."

"No, Ma'am, you don't understand."

"Oh, yes I do, I do understand."

"No, you don't know. You haven't gone out to where the body shop was and seen the cars that are parked outside there."

"Well, if you know those cars are there, why don't you do something about it?"

Alma Trinidad knows the answer. Yes, they are afraid, but that is not the full reason.

"The authorities are good for nothing," she told me. "But I would also say they are involved, because how else can you explain that two years have gone by and they've done nothing? For them it's 'They already killed your son; now go home and cry.' Why? Why do we have to do that? If that's the case then they should leave too. If they are so useless, they should get out of here."

And yet she finds the same response everywhere she goes. The judges in charge of the case told her early on, "Don't get your hopes up." But she continues.

She and César went to the state office for victims of violent crime. They had an appointment with the staff psychologist. The waiting room was empty. When the psychologist came out and ushered them into her office she said, "Let's make this quick, because it's not free. And no tears." She then gave them a food basket with cooking oil and rice, valued at about ten dollars. Alma Trinidad looked the psychologist in the eyes and said, "You know, if you actually helped people the line would stretch out this building and down to Obregón Avenue. But people must know that you are useless and that's why you're alone here." She and César left and sought help from a private psychologist.

She filed a complaint with the Sinaloa State Human Rights Commission. The result?

"The State Human Rights Commission forged my signature on a document officially closing my case as resolved, as if I had been fully informed and in agreement that they close it," she said.

The state human rights workers forged her signature? I asked her what happened next.

"Nothing," she answered. "Nothing happened. Here in Sinaloa nothing happens. Come on, they kill us and nothing happens, what's going to happen with a forged signature?"

Once when she went to review her son's case file the homicide detective said, "Ma'am, we've now identified the weapons that killed your son in the workshop." It turns out that those same weapons have been used in another twenty-plus crimes and killed more than sixty other people.

Alma Trinidad was not impressed. "How can you not be ashamed to tell me that? How can you not be ashamed? What do I gain with you having identified the weapons if you haven't arrested the killers? They're out there killing and killing. What are you waiting for, for them to show up and kill someone here? Or what are you waiting for? How is it possible that you know they are out there killing and killing and you don't go arrest them?"

For Alma Trinidad learned, through her dogged reading of case files—which as the relative of a murder victim she has full access to under Mexican law—that the authorities actually know the names and addresses of her son's killers. In one of the sworn testimonies in another unsolved homicide case involving the same weapons, the brother of a murder victim testified who the killers are and where they live. No arrest warrant has been issued for these gunmen; no homicide detective has gone to pay them a visit, ask them a few questions.

"There is no law here," she told me, "Culiacán is a place without law. Or rather, there is law for the highest bidder, for whoever can pay the most. Justice for the highest bidder."

She knows this and still she demands that those who speak in the name of the law do their jobs.

Alma Trinidad together with other mothers of other young people gunned down in the streets formed a nonprofit organization called Voices United for Life (*Voces Unidas por la Vida*) to demand justice for their children. In one case the attorney general claimed that the young man in question had committed suicide.

"They said that he killed himself," she said. "They found him wrapped in a blanket and black tape, and the boy committed suicide. I mean, they think people are dumb. They think people are stupid, that they are dealing with people as idiotic as they are, because you can't describe them any other way. Come on, they say that the boy committed suicide when someone had thrown him in a canal wrapped in a blanket and electrical tape. Suicide. The boy shot himself, wrapped himself up, and threw himself into a canal. Yes. Just like that. Really."

She and the other women began to march, hold rallies and protests in front of state and municipal government buildings, and every two weeks go there to demand progress in their investigations. "Even if we just go to say hello, because they never have any new leads in the case, never have done any work, we don't stop going. Every two weeks."

They spent two years requesting an interview with Sinaloa governor Jesús Alberto Aguilar Padilla before his office granted them a meeting. "We thought that if we were able to speak directly with him, then perhaps things would change a little bit, that they would do something about catching the criminals. But now we see that no. We had the meeting and things are exactly the same."

They requested a meeting with the famed senator Rosario Ibarra de Piedra. Ibarra de Piedra became an activist in 1974 when federal agents "disappeared" her son, Jesús Piedra Ibarra, who was accused of being a member of the urban guerrilla group Communist League of September 23. In 1977, Ibarra de Piedra founded the Committee for the Defense of Political Prisoners, the Persecuted, the Disappeared, and Exiles, known as Comité ¡Eureka!. Ibarra de Piedra was an icon of resistance to the PRI regime and fought for years against the official cover-up of those killed and disappeared during Mexico's repression of both armed and unarmed protest movements in the 1970s. In 2006, Ibarra de Piedra became a senator under the Mexican system of assigning a certain number of seats in the senate and chamber of deputies based on the number of seats won in the election. So Alma Trinidad and her colleagues saved up, scrambled to get a week off from their jobs and from the chores of their homes, and traveled to Mexico City. Ibarra de Piedra received them in her office, gave them the numbers of her legal team, and said good-bye. When the mothers of Voices United for Life called the numbers, they received only two alternating kinds of advice; leave a message or call back later.

"Well, we thought of Rosario Ibarra de Piedra as a mother," Alma Trinidad said, "because she lived through a situation similar to ours, they disappeared her son, we thought she would help us, but no. And so we understood that the lady is no longer a mother; now she is a senator."

So much rejection, so many closed doors, so many months and then years that go by with nothing to show for their efforts. "It is demoralizing," she said, "And I think they do it with this in mind. They want people to see that there are no possibilities. They want them to go off and stop looking for justice. Why should people go on if the authorities will do nothing? It is very difficult; it is not easy at all." Several of the other women in the group, in fact, have started to pull away; they do not want to go on.

Alma Trinidad goes on. On the two-year anniversary of the Mega 2000 massacre she held a rally in Culiacán's main square. She printed a black banner with dozens of names in white: all innocent people gunned down in the drug war in Culiacán. She baked a three-tiered black cake with red candles and called it the Impunity Cake, for the only thing the government has given them to celebrate, she said, is impunity for the killers.

Some people tell her that she should give up too, for her own safety, and that anyway, "God will do justice one day." To this her response is vehement.

"Well, what do we want justice on Earth for, then? If we're just going to sit around and wait for justice in heaven, then what do we want these good-for-nothings here for?" she says of the detectives and lawyers, judges, state psychologists and human rights commissioners, senators and governors, attorney generals and presidents, people who cash their paychecks in the name of justice on Earth. "Well, even if all is lost, I'm going to make their lives impossible."

Here is the genius of Alma Trinidad's rebellion in the land of impunity: where everyone tells her justice is impossible, she says okay, then I will continue to insist on justice, and in so doing make your life impossible. That spirit is what hope looks like in a place where murder is the local, everyday by-product of the global industry that caters to people who get high.

Alma Trinidad's rebellion began on the day of her son's murder. She rebelled against the mutilation of her son. She refused to look at Cristóbal, to identify him, see him in the morgue, or see him in the coffin. Not after what they did to him. She refused to let the bullets tear into her son's tender

16-year-old face a second time, in her memories. The gunman, possibly the same age or only a few years older than Cristóbal, had shot him through the hand, which apparently Cristóbal had extended to stop the bullets in a desperate last clinging to life. The gunman then shot him at close range in the face and head, with high-caliber bullets, the impact of which can lift your body in the air and toss it to the ground. César had failed to notice at first due to the way Cristóbal had fallen and then finally collapsed. When he went to lift him up, he saw.

"I didn't want to see Cristóbal," Alma told me. "I wanted to remember him as he was. I felt that if I looked at him as he had been left, that I would have been worse, that I would have gone crazy. I think it is the best thing I could have done. Now my son comes into my mind with a smile, as he was, a beautiful boy. That's how I remember him."

THREE

The city belongs to them.
—Rafael

BEFORE THE *COMANDANTE* SAID, "Take these guys and ice 'em," before they put a black hood over his head and closed the doors, before they forced him down and placed the barrel of a 9mm pistol against the back of his head, before that moment, Rafael still had hope. And hope is everything.

Everyone was talking about Reynosa, the city of half a million people across the border from McAllen, Texas. There were tales of roadblocks and gun battles, tales of executions, of bodies in the streets. It was February 2010 and gun battles, executions, and dumped bodies had become the norm in many parts of Mexico. Something different was happening in Reynosa. All the talking took place inside a chamber of silence. There were no official statements, no local news reports, and no national or international correspondents on the scene, no photographs, no radio interviews, no documentation, only talk. A friend said the city was under siege.

A friend of a friend said people were afraid to go outside. Someone heard that the schools were empty; parents terrified that their children would get caught in the crossfire on their way to school were keeping them at home. In late February 2010 the U.S. Consulate in Reynosa closed its office until further notice. Reynosa residents anonymously posted accounts of gun battles on Twitter. Everyone was talking about Reynosa, but the talk was all off camera, off the record. The governor of Tamaulipas said that "collective paranoia" was to blame. A woman then posted a video recorded with her cell phone to YouTube. Off camera the woman said, "The government says it is paranoia." The video showed two lifeless bodies, shot-up SUVs, hundreds of bullet casings on the pavement, deserted streets and stores, and in the distance Mexican soldiers standing by. A reporter told me that the woman was later dragged from her home and killed.

Rafael is not given to paranoia. At 30 he carries himself with an unusual air of sustained concentration. When you speak with him, you can *see* him thinking. He works for Milenio TV in Mexico City and is an exhaustive reporter. He is in Monterrey, Mexico's northern financial capital and the city where he earned an undergraduate degree in journalism and worked for several years. He is on vacation; his mobile phone rings, and he answers. His boss is on the line and says, "You know what, man, there have been a bunch of shoot-outs in Reynosa, but nobody knows what's going on. We want you to head over there and document what you can."

Rafael takes a bus to Reynosa. On the way into town the bus stops at a police roadblock. Several officers board the bus and scan the passengers. The only person they speak to is Rafael.

"Identification, please."

Rafael hands them his ID and press credentials. He thinks, "Why just me? Is it the way I look?"

The police hand him back his ID and press card, get off the bus, and wave it on.

The bus pulls into the station and Rafael is gathering his bags when his cell rings.

"Rafa, are you in Reynosa?"

"Yes."

"Um, well, we want to let you know that Multimedios has a problem there in Reynosa," says his boss. Multimedios is Milenio TV's parent company. "There seems to be a cameraman on staff there who works for . . . the bad guys. We just wanted to give you the tip so you can take precautions."

Rafael hangs up. He knew he was traveling into a place controlled by the Gulf Cartel and the Zetas, but he thought he could at least count on the national media company he works for to provide support and contacts via the office in Reynosa. Not so. He calls the Milenio news director in Reynosa, a friend whom he knows to be an honest reporter, and says, "Hey, I'm at the bus station. Come pick me up."

In the car they talk. The news director says things are very heavy here. Milenio, along with the other news outlets, he says, has published next to nothing about it. The cartels

control the local media. Not all reporters are on the take, but
those who are honest are terrified. Drug lords impose censorship with cash, fear, or death, but whichever way it's done,
it is absolute. What cannot be said is never said. The news
director confirms that the cameraman in question works for
a cartel. Milenio has sent a cameraman from Mexico City
who will be arriving at the Reynosa airport shortly. Rafael
decides not to work out of the Reynosa office. He decides to
stay at a different hotel each day.

Rafael has not accepted the reign of censorship. His
editor sent him to Reynosa to document what he can. He
is a reporter and that is what he has come to do. He is not
careless, nor fearless. He does not have a death wish. He
is not an adrenaline junky. He is a measured person. He is
not a war correspondent; he has never been to a war zone.
But now his editors have sent him to report on gun battles
that no one else is covering. And he plans to do so. But he
is not stupid. He knows that you cannot be seen reporting
on a gun battle, you cannot stand on a street corner with
your camera running. If you do that you will be shot dead if
you're lucky, taken off and put through hideous torture and
then killed if you're not.

A few days before Rafael arrived, a convoy of cartel gunmen attacked the Reynosa prison in an attempt to
break out some of their cohorts. Brazen prisoner breakouts
are common in the drug war zones. In May 2009, some
thirty gunmen traveling in a convoy of seventeen vehicles
with a helicopter flying overhead raided a state prison in

Cieneguillas, Zacatecas. The gunmen, some in federal police uniforms, pulled up before dawn, marched into the prison without firing a shot, demanded that the prison guards release fifty-three inmates, including eleven considered highly dangerous by Interpol, and then marched the prisoners—some of whom could not conceal their grins—out to the waiting vehicles, whereupon they drove off into the night. Before leaving, however, they broke into a prison storage room and stole twenty-three guns. The entire operation took two minutes and fifty-two seconds. Security cameras recorded the whole thing. Within days the prison director and all forty-four on-duty guards were themselves jailed for questioning. In Reynosa, the breakout attempt did not go so smoothly. Gunmen attacked and prison guards fought back. The gun battle lasted some two hours, until the attackers finally gave up and left without freeing any of the convicts.

Rafael and his cameraman, Eduardo, fresh off the plane from Mexico City, decide to go out to the prison to film the bullet holes in the walls and guard towers. No one wants to speak with them, much less in front of the camera.

They go to interview the mayor of Reynosa. He admits that things have become "difficult" in town. The city government has recently opened a Twitter account to inform residents of the locations of gun battles throughout town. Rafael thinks that in itself is a story, though perhaps a marginal one. So he asks the mayor about the Twitter account and about the locations of various gun battles over the previous few days. He and Eduardo produce a small

segment on the Twitter account and the bullet holes out at
the Reynosa prison and send it off to Mexico City.

No one wants to speak with them. That makes reporting
next to impossible. But Rafael does not give up; he does not
stay in his hotel room. Their second day in town, Rafael and
Eduardo decide to just head out and drive around for a bit.
Eduardo drives and Rafael is checking Twitter on his mobile phone when they hear a police siren behind them. They
are in downtown Reynosa, near the city government offices.
They glance back and notice how traffic parts behind them
to make way for the police car to pass. They pull over as
well. But as they do, they see that the siren does not emit
from a police car, but rather from a grey Jeep Cherokee with
tinted windows, strobe headlights similar to those used by
police vehicles, and a turret with a mounted machine gun.
The Cherokee has no front license plate, but as it passes,
Rafael sees that it has a back license plate that reads CDG,
the Spanish acronym for the Gulf Cartel (*Cartel del Golfo*).
The Cherokee speeds past blasting its siren and is followed
by nine luxury SUVs—Suburbans, Escalades, Yukons—some
without plates, others with plates from the Gulf of Mexico
states of Veracruz and Tamaulipas. Some also bear the letters
CDG painted with white shoe polish on the sides or back
windows. In each of these nine SUVs men with assault rifles
hover in the open windows with their weapons at ready. The
convoy speeds by and turns a few blocks up ahead.

Rafael looks to Eduardo and says, "Let's follow them,
but discreetly."

And so they do. They make the same turn up ahead and find the convoy already parked in front of a restaurant in downtown Reynosa, right behind City Hall. The gunmen get out and walk into the restaurant, fully armed, apparently making a lunch stop.

Rafael and Eduardo drive by and keep going.

The scene makes an impression on Rafael. He thinks, "Now that is tangible evidence of impunity, of the fact that they are the ones in charge of Reynosa. They can drive in convoys, hanging out the windows with assault rifles, and no one says a thing."

Rafael meets up with a friend who knows the town. He asks him who controls the *plaza* in Reynosa. The friend gives him the name: Samuel Flores Borrego, alias Metro Tres. Rafael types the name into an Internet search engine. He finds an entry on Borrego on the U.S. Department of State's Narcotics Rewards Programs website. Borrego is 37 years old, weighs 155 pounds, stands five feet nine inches tall. He is a "ranking member of the Gulf Cartel and is currently in control of Cartel operations in Reynosa and Miguel Alemán, Mexico," according to the website.

The U.S. Department of State is offering $5 million for information that leads to Borrego's arrest. Rafael keeps searching. He types in "Metro Tres" and is led to a video on YouTube. He listens. The song, by the Reynosa hip-hop duo Cano and Blunt, is called simply *The Song of Metro Tres*. The lyrics praise Metro Tres for his ferocity and loyalty: "He was a government official / now he's in the gang / and he's got hella people under his command." One of the repeated verses says: "Straight up people, we tell it like it is; this is dedicated to Metro Tres / one of the good ones, he reigns over his territory / with a nine and an AK, he sends you to hell." The video consists of a handful of still images of Cano and Blunt in various mafia outfits striking gangster poses. In one of the photographs they pose with a number of other men in front of a mural of themselves.

This, Rafael thinks, is a story. The world of drug trafficking so deeply imbedded in popular culture and everyday life that local musicians compose and self-publish songs about the gangster in charge of their hometown *plaza*. Though there is a longstanding tradition of such compositions in the form of traditional *corridos*, Cano and Blunt represent the latest trend in hip-hop narco-music. "I need to find this group," Rafael thinks. He asks around about where he might find the rapper mural he saw online and is directed to a low-income neighborhood where most residents work in the border maquiladoras. There he asks where he might find the muralist and the two rappers in the mural. After a bit of walking around he and Eduardo stand before them.

Cano and Blunt come from hard streets and have crafted a hard look: shaved heads, dark glasses, and baggy shirts, flashing gang signals, hanging out in a luxury SUV. In one of their YouTube videos they pose with a cute, two-foot-tall stuffed rabbit. Cano holds the rabbit by its ears, pulling its head back, while Blunt aims a stockless AK-47 assault rifle at the bunny's forehead. In one of their songs,

Reynosa la Maldosa (roughly, Reynosa the Wicked) they sing this chorus: "We are pure Reynosa, a fuckload of thugs / pure mafiosos, suffer it or enjoy it / Reynosa the wicked, the street is dangerous / look alive, pure mafiosos."

Cano and Blunt are not happy to see Rafael and Eduardo. They repeatedly ask them who they are, what they are doing, why they have sought them out. Rafael explains, but his explanations do little to ease the suspicion. He says he'll come back tomorrow. He does. This time they agree to an interview but say that they will not talk about their "dedicated songs," referring to those praising specific figures in the drug-trafficking underworld like Borrego, el Metro Tres. In the interview Cano and Blunt sit on a concrete block in front of the mural of themselves. It is night. They talk about new generations who no longer listen to *corridos* but prefer reggaeton and hip-hop. Cano says of the song *Reynosa la Maldosa*, "We see what the street is like, what's going down, and our song is about that. That's it. That's what's happening and that's where we get our inspiration."

When the interview is over and the camera turned off they speak a bit more frankly. One says about their dedicated songs, "We've never met the people we write about. But there are people who show up at my house and give me three hundred dollars and say they want me to write a song about one guy or another and that the song should more or less say this and that. And we try to be creative and give it good rhyme so that it'll be catchy." Rafael and Eduardo go back to the hotel, edit, and send a three-minute news clip

about narco hip-hop that includes playing a few verses of
The Song of Metro Tres over images of shot-up SUVs, police
roadblocks, and military convoys.

Rafael and Eduardo are waiting for an interview with
the commander of the military base in Reynosa. They are
television reporters, so they need images. Rafael says, "Let's
go film the police roadblock out on the highway on the way
into town." They drive out and park about 200 yards away
to shoot initial images from a distance. While filming from
inside their rental car, they notice a group of police jump
into a truck and head toward them at top speed. Within seconds they arrive, arms drawn and aimed.

"Get out of the car! Hands on the dash!"

"Easy, we're press," Rafael says as he complies. "We're
press. Here are our credentials. We're from Mexico City."

The police officer in charge reviews their credentials
and then says, "Sorry about that, things here are very tense.
Very tense."

Now with permission, they drive up closer. Eduardo
films the roadblock from various angles while Rafael talks
with the police commander, who begins to speak with what
might appear uncharacteristic candor for the police.

"Look, what we want is to get the Zetas the fuck out of
here," he says. "All they do is commit barbarities among the
civilian population, and we don't want them here."

But this is still in code. Rafael begins to understand.
The police are working with the Gulf Cartel. The roadblock is to either stop Zeta gunmen from entering Reynosa,

or if overpowered, to tip off the CDG about any Zeta convoy arrivals. The gun battles raging in Reynosa are part of
an open war between the Gulf Cartel and the Zetas, their
former employees, fighting for control over the *plaza*. Just
the other day Rafael had seen a *narcomanta*, a huge banner
hung from an overpass that read: THE UNION OF CARTELS IS
NOW HERE TO ELIMINATE THE ZETAS. AUTHORITIES, WE ASK
THAT YOU NOT GET INVOLVED. VENOM MUST BE FOUGHT WITH
VENOM. The police commander made clear that they were
complying with the Gulf Cartel's request, maintaining roadblocks on the outskirts of town, and leaving the gun battles
to the CDG.

Rafael and Eduardo have been in Reynosa for five days and
they have stayed in five different hotels. Rafael gets up in
the morning of the sixth day and checks his email. He has
a message describing how a local reporter was taken to the
hospital the previous night because he had fallen into a "dia-
betic coma," but it turns out he had severe wounds all over
his body from a beating. He died at the hospital, shortly
after being admitted. Another email says that two reporters with Reynosa's largest daily paper, *El Mañana de Reynosa*,
are missing. Rafael writes down the names of these three
reporters in his notebook and starts to call around. He finds
the name and number for the deceased reporter's wife and
calls her. She says, "I can't talk to you right now; I can't give
you an interview. We are on our way to Tampico to bury
my husband." He calls the editorial desk at *El Mañana de*

Reynosa to ask for the two journalists reported missing. He does not mention their possible disappearance, but simply asks for them by name. The receptionist says, "No, they haven't come in yet."

Rafael checks his email again and sees that people are starting to send Twitter messages about a gunfight in a neighborhood in Reynosa. Rafael says, "Well, let's go look for this gunfight, no? See if we can get some images of what has happened." They go out to their rental car, a red Volkswagen Jetta with Coahuila plates, and head out. They changed rental cars the day before after hearing rumors that a convoy of Zetas had arrived in town from Coahuila state. They had been driving an SUV with Coahuila plates and decided it would be best to get a different car. Unfortunately all the vehicles at the rental agency had Coahuila plates, but at least a red Jetta would not immediately look like a satellite unit from a Zeta death squad.

They get in the car and head out toward the neighborhood where the Twitter messages had reported the shootout. They are driving through downtown, Eduardo at the wheel, Rafael checking Twitter on his mobile. They stop at a major intersection and look up to see a CDG convoy pass right in front of them. About seven Suburban-type SUVs traveling at top speed with armed men hovering in the windows. They decide to go straight and then turn right two blocks up ahead. But as they turn they see the convoy parked alongside an outdoor public square, right there in front of them. The men are out of their vehicles, putting on their bulletproof vests, loading their assault rifle clips, preparing for battle. Rafa and Eduardo drive on, but they notice that the men are watching them. And then they hear a whistle and a shout, "Go get them!"

Eduardo speeds up and turns. Then he floors it and turns again. And then an SUV passes them and cuts them off. Eduardo brakes and five men jump out wearing bulletproof vests and aiming AR-15 assault rifles. They shout, "Get out of the car! Get the fuck out, assholes!"

Rafael says to Eduardo, "We're fucked." Then they get out.

One gunman says, "What are you fucks up to, eh?"

Rafael holds his press credential out and says, "We're reporters."

The men surround them and take their press credentials. One says, "Get in the truck. We'll take your car. Give me the keys."

Eduardo gives him the keys and they get in. Rafael notices the plush leather seats.

The gunmen tear off, back to the parked convoy. Two follow in the red Jetta. Traffic parts around them. One says to Rafael and Eduardo, "You guys are done. We're going to fuck you up."

They pull up and park. Gunmen approach on both sides and open the doors, forcing Rafael and Eduardo out on each side. They frisk them and remove all their belongings: wallets, notebooks, and mobile phones, which they turn off. Another group of gunmen begins to extract everything from the red Jetta, opening the glove compartment, the trunk, checking under the hood, gathering their computers, backpacks, cameras, everything. The gunmen ask if they have a satellite-tracking device in the car, and they say no.

Once the gunmen take all their possessions they force Rafael and Eduardo to get back in the SUV, each sitting on one side facing their interrogators, who stand gathered around the doors, weapons pointed straight at them. The gunmen all wear bulletproof vests with CDG stitched over the chest. They carry extra clips for their guns and some have grenades hanging from their vests; some carry radio equipment. All carry AR-15 assault rifles and most also have a 9mm pistol strapped to their thighs.

A thick man, about five feet nine inches tall, with a flame tattoo on his neck, stands before Rafael. He carries only an AR-15. A thinner man stands guard slightly behind him with an AR-15 ready and a pistol in its holster.

The interrogation begins.

"Who are you and what the fuck are you doing here?"

Rafael answers, "We are reporters for Milenio TV in Mexico City."

"Where are you from?"

Eduardo answers, "I'm from Mexico City," and the gunman with rage in his eyes standing before him says, "Ah? Chilango?" and begins to hit him in the face and body.

Rafael, from a northern state known for drug production and trafficking, lets the question slide and luckily the gunman with the flame tattoo does not pursue it.

"What are you doing here," he asks Rafael.

"We came to report on the Twitter account that City Hall has opened to inform residents about the gun battles."

"Bullshit."

And here the comandante arrives, the boss of this troop. Rafael sees him and thinks, "This guy's a Rambo, a Blackwater mercenary." Like the others, the comandante wears a bulletproof vest and a 9mm pistol on his thigh. He holds an AR-15 assault rifle, but he uses two *huevos del toro*, ammo drums capable of holding up to 150 rounds. The comandante's arms are hugely muscular. On one arm he has a tattoo of a woman's silhouette. He wears black combat boots and fatigues and a military haircut.

"What are you doing here?" the comandante demands. "You guys are Zetas."

"We're reporters," Rafael begins to answer.

"No, you guys are federal police. You guys are soldiers, you're from the army. You're here to betray us. But you know what? We're going to give you the opportunity to tell us the truth."

"We are telling you the truth. We're reporters from Mexico City here to cover this story."

And with that the beating begins. The comandante walks over to the other side of the SUV where they are beating Eduardo. The thick gunman with the tattooed neck beats Rafael. Punches to the face. Slaps to the face. Open palm slaps over the ears. Punches using the side of the fist against the neck, hitting the carotid artery.

"What are you doing here? Tell us the truth! You're lying!"

"I'm telling you the truth."

"Hand me the nine. This guy doesn't get it," the gunman says to the man standing behind him. "Hand me the nine, I left mine back at the house."

He takes the pistol, chambers a bullet, and presses it into Rafael's ribs.

"Tell me the truth or you will die right here, asshole."

"I'm telling you the truth. We are reporters, believe me sir," Rafael says. "There are our IDs and press credentials. On the back is the phone number for the news desk. Call and confirm that we were sent here from Mexico City. Please." Rafael's voice shakes and cracks.

"Why is your voice cracking, asshole?"

"Because you've got a pistol pressed into me and you're threatening me," Rafael answers with the precision of a trained reporter.

The gunman raises the pistol and slams the stock down against Rafael's knee. Again. And Again. "You guys are a bunch of pansy-ass bitches," he says.

The comandante walks back over to Rafael's side and flips through Rafael's notebook. "Why do you have the telephone numbers for the public security chief in Reynosa?" he asks.

"Because I wanted to interview him."

Rafael looks at the comandante when he answers him. A mistake.

"What the fuck are you looking at punk? Don't look at my face!"

Rafael quickly looks down.

"What is up with these names?" he asks, seeing the names of the disappeared journalists Rafael had written down that morning. "What do you want to know? Why do you have these names here?"

"Well, those are the names of some journalists that friends gave me to contact for information since I don't know the situation here," Rafael answers, not wanting to mention that he had heard reports of their disappearance.

"No, these guys are up to no good. Fuck 'em up, handcuff 'em and ice 'em," the comandante says. "Take these guys and ice 'em."

They put black hoods over their heads. They handcuff Eduardo, but can't find a second pair for Rafael. The gunmen get in the backseat with them, close the doors and drive. Now Rafael knows he will die. This is when he loses hope. He is a dead man waiting only for the last moments. He thinks, "Holy fuck. We're screwed." He stares into the pitch darkness of the thick hood placed over him: "This is all that follows; nothing, permanent black and that's it. I hope they don't torture me and that they leave my body in a public place. The fucking anguish of families that live with having someone disappeared; that kills families. I hope they leave my body where it can be found."

A call to the gunmen's radio pierces his thoughts; he hears a voice say, "Tell them to get them down!" And hands force his head down into his lap and he feels the barrel of a gun press into the back of his skull. But Rafael is a dead man now and thus is no longer ruined by fear. He starts to listen to the gunmen's radio communications. He hears calls coming in from other CDG gunmen reporting on the locations of both army and Zetas convoys, and reporting on their own movements throughout the city.

The drive does not take long, five or seven minutes. They stop. Rafael hears a large door opening, and then they drive though and the door closes. The gunmen take them out and sit them down in chairs. And the interrogation begins again. Where are you from? What are you doing here? Are you soldiers? Are you Zetas? Tell the truth! If you don't tell the truth you will die.

Eduardo begins to fidget. The handcuffs have cut off the circulation to his hands.

"Stop moving, bitch!" And someone kicks Eduardo in the stomach.

"What the fuck are you doing here? Who are you?"

"We are reporters," Rafael says.

"Bullshit! You are soldiers."

"We are reporters," Rafael repeats.

"No, you are Zetas. You're federal police. You've come to turn us in."

Rafael knows that the voices he hears through the hood can disappear him there in the house and no one would ever know what happened. Rafael feels like he is talking to God. The voices have all the power to kill, release, torture, or whatever else they may feel like doing with them. He only speaks when spoken to. He only answers those questions put to him directly and then he answers precisely, truthfully, without sarcasm or aggression, without unsolicited information.

The comandante asks, "Who is Rafael?"

"I am."

"You're the smart one, right? You're the one in charge?"

"No, sir, I am a reporter."

"No, you're the tough motherfucker they send all over the place, right? You go wherever there's action, right?"

"No, sir." Rafael thinks of responding, "No sir, I'm the idiot who says yes and accepts the assignment," but he holds back.

The comandante asks, "Who is this general?"

"I don't know," Rafael responds, "I can't see."

"Don't be a fucking idiot. Who is this general?"

"Let me see." They lift his hood and Rafael sees the comandante holding Rafael's camera out to him with a photograph of an army general on the screen. Rafael does not look at the comandante's face.

"That is the general in charge of the November 20 military parade. I interviewed him before the parade."

Eduardo keeps moving involuntarily, adjusting his hands, his arms, his back, trying to release the pressure in his wrists, but also trembling all over. A gunman shouts, "Why are you shaking punk?" Eduardo says, "Because I am afraid."

One of the gunmen going through Rafael's things speaks

up from across the room. "This guy has a whole fuck of a lot of shit on his computer," he says, "documents from the Attorney General's office, army documents, he's got photos of Beltrán Leyva."

"Why," the comandante asks, "do you have photos of Beltrán Leyva?"

"Because I went to cover the operation. I am assigned to cover security issues. They sent me and I went."

"So you are the badass they send all over the place?"

"No."

The comandante and his soldiers continue to look through Rafael's computer, camera, and notebook and talk amongst themselves. Then they pick up a radio and call, "Hey, we've got two reporters here who say they're from Mexico City, from Milenio or whatever the fuck." They wait for the response and it comes.

The comandante turns back to them, "How much did you have in your wallet?"

Rafael says about a thousand pesos ($75). The comandante checks to see if the money is still there; it is.

"Look," the comandante says to his two hooded captives, "Your things are all here. We are not street rats. We don't want you coming here because all you do is say pure bullshit and heat up the *plaza*. We do not want to see you here, assfucks. We're going to let you go, but we do not want to see you here because you heat up the *plaza*. And don't even think about publishing that we kidnapped you because we are present in every state in the country and if we want to we can kill you anywhere in the country. Nothing happened here."

When he hears the words "We're going to let you go," Rafael realizes that he is still alive. He had been a dead man for a few hours, and those words give him life again, and with that life, hope.

The gunmen lead them back into the SUV, still hooded. They drive for some fifteen minutes and then park. They remove Eduardo's handcuffs; they remove the hoods from both men. They open the doors and lead them out. They are standing in front of a pharmacy. Their rental car is parked right next to them with the keys in the ignition. Rafael and Eduardo stand there, dumbstruck, unable to move. Rafael feels a strange, somewhat insidious urge to thank the man with the tattooed neck who had interrogated and beaten him for hours; he thinks of giving this man his watch.

And the man shouts, "Go suck dick, bitches! Get the fuck out of here!"

"Thank you," Rafael says, "thank you very much."

They walk to the car, get in, start the ignition, and floor it. They head for their hotel to get the rest of their things. Rafael turns on his mobile phone and calls his editor in Mexico City. "We got picked up by the narcos," he says, "I'm headed to Monterrey, now. Fuck this." He hangs up. He becomes aware of the aching pain in his knees from where the gunman repeatedly beat him with the pistol. Two minutes later his phone rings. His editor says, "Don't go to Monterrey, go straight to the airport, the director of Milenio just got off the phone with the federal police and they are sending a unit to stand guard until the flight leaves."

They drive to the airport and take the first flight out to Mexico City. Upon arriving they talk to the top editors at Milenio and tell them what happened. The editors are extremely worried. Rafael says, "I don't want my name or anything linked to my name out there. If you want to write about this, denounce what happened, don't mention me."

Ciro Gómez Leyva, the Milenio news director responsible for sending the crew to Reynosa, will write in his column, "Every day in more regions in Mexico it is impossible to do reporting. Journalism is dead in Reynosa."

A few days later, Alfredo Corchado of the *Dallas Morning News* travels to Reynosa to report on the story of disappeared journalists. While he is filming street scenes with a television crew from Belo Television, a stranger approaches him and says, "You have no permission to report here. It's best you leave now."

Corchado files his story, "Cartels use intimidation campaigns to stifle news coverage in Mexico," and leaves town. Months later, the two journalists kidnapped while Rafael was in town are still disappeared, along with three others.

I spoke with Rafael in Monterrey several months after he and Eduardo were *levantados* and miraculously released. Just days before we met, Monterrey had been completely paralyzed by gun battles and *narco-bloqueos*, the drug gang practice of stopping motorists at gunpoint, taking their cars, and using them to shut off major avenues and thus impede enemy cartel, police, or army pursuit. The gunmen favor eighteen-wheelers and city buses but use any and all vehicles on the road. Often the gunmen lie in wait to ambush their pursuers. Gun battles rage throughout the city.

Monterrey, with a greater metropolitan population of more than 4 million people, is Mexico's second-largest city after Mexico City. The wealthiest municipality in the country is San Pedro Garza García, one of the municipalities making up the greater metropolitan area and the headquarters of Monterrey's business elite. For many years, Mexico's drug lords quietly bought property in San Pedro and kept their families there. Some of Mexico's largest transnational corporations are based there, such as Cemex, the third-largest concrete company in the world, and FEMSA, Mexico's largest beverage company and owner of the OXXO convenience store chain, again, the biggest such chain in the country. Far from being a dusty, forgotten border town, Monterrey is the poster image of Mexico's "free trade" ideal of development: towering skyscrapers, sweeping plazas surrounded by art museums, glitzy shopping malls, bustling nightclub districts, elite private schools and universities. Monterrey represents the myth that the Mexican elite likes to tell itself about the country's future. From the hills of San Pedro Garza García everything looks shiny. For many in Monterrey the drug war was as distant and abstract as the economic destitution in which half of Mexico's people live.

In 2010, with the split between the Gulf Cartel and

the Zetas, things changed. Monterrey became yet another urban battlefield. In mid-March, drug gangs shut down the highways leading in and out of town, blocked some thirty major avenues and streets in the metropolitan area, and engaged in pitched gun battles with each other, the federal police, the army, and the navy. In one gunfight two young graduate students at Mexico's top-ranked private university, the Tecnológico de Monterrey, were slain in the street. Army soldiers hid their student IDs, planted guns on them, and later told the press that they were Zetas. Almost immediately their true identities were discovered—Jorge Antonio Mercado Alonso, 23, and Javier Francisco Arredondo Verdugo, 24, both on full scholarship for academic excellence—and the news of their killing and the Mexican army's botched cover-up became a national scandal. Consuelo Morales, the director of Citizens in Support of Human Rights in Monterrey, told reporter Sanjuana Martínez at the time, "We are swallowing the idea that everyone the military kills is a criminal, and that is what they tried to make us believe with the Tec students, who they said at first were hit men and planted guns on them. But since the students were from a certain social class, the theater did not work for the army."

In April 2010, seventy-eight people were gunned down in Monterrey, the highest monthly execution tally in the city's history up to that point. In one case, some fifty gunmen blocked several downtown streets and then stormed a Holiday Inn, demanding at gunpoint that the front desk clerk search the hotel records for a list of names. Once the gunmen had the room numbers of those they were looking for, they proceeded to go up to the fifth floor, pull five people from their rooms, march them out of the hotel, grab a clerk from another hotel across the street, and drive off. Those six people have not been seen since. In May 2010, there was another wave of *narco-bloqueos*, leading prominent business executives to take out advertisements in the daily newspapers demanding an end to such impunity.

Between August 13 and 17, 2010, the Gulf Cartel and the Zetas again engaged in open warfare throughout Monterrey. Drug gangs blocked some forty streets and avenues, threw grenades at businesses and television stations, fought gun battles in the streets, and summarily executed more than ten people, including the mayor of Santiago, one of the eleven municipalities making up metropolitan Monterrey.

By June 2010 the eruptions of urban warfare and drugland executions reached such a level that the arrival of Hurricane Alex with its 110-mile-per-hour winds and pounding rain was greeted as a respite from the gunplay.

"Alex was a break for us; we could do journalism again," said Luis Petersen, the director of Multimedia in Monterrey, a media company that publishes the regional daily newspaper *Milenio Monterrey* and broadcasts throughout the northwest on more than thirty radio stations and two major television stations. "It was a break for the state government as well. The governor, ten months after taking office, could in fact finally assume office. He went out to the affected villages and spoke to people on the ground. He could work on actually solving a problem. That lasted about two weeks."

Luis and I drove through Monterrey one day in late August as rumors circulated that a convoy of forty SUVs bringing Zetas reinforcements into town had just arrived. I asked him how one should cover the drug war.

"We can't do journalism here anymore," he told me. "For me it is very difficult to do journalism when you have to take sides from the outset. It seems that we have to do that here, and the side to take is that of an institution in danger, the Mexican state. It is in the hands of people without broad popular support; the only thing they have is firepower. The twenty years of Mexican struggles for a democratic opening . . . that doesn't exist anymore. Who exercises sovereignty? Where is power located? It is in the hands of *those* people. And the police? Infiltrated.

"So we can't do journalism. Why? Because we have to have a preconceived stance. Here's an example. The army does not recognize its errors, which means deaths. And they are not going to recognize them and we can't force them to. In the case of the Tec students, we can't say it was the army's fault. Why? Because we are choosing to favor them."

Luis received a call on his cell. "We are calling it a detention," he said. He paused, and then: "They are asking us to not publish anything yet." He glanced at me and gestured at his cell as if saying, "See what I mean?" After a bit he hung up and said, "That's it. The army is asking me not to publish information about a shoot-out that happened today. The army is not asking me directly; the state government is doing the asking. There is no way. We can't do journalism here.

"The state governments have been defeated through the infiltration of their police forces. The municipal governments are defeated. Business leaders are defeated."

"How do you understand this war?" I asked him.

"The government lost control. This war is a war to regain control of drug trafficking from the perspective of the state. And this, to me, isn't necessarily a bad thing. Drug trafficking isn't going to go away. Perhaps the only deep, long-term solution would be to legalize, and from that position control many aspects, not just the violence, but health issues as well. Why not legalize drugs? It seems to me that there are many people for whom it is much better for drugs to remain illegal."

Three days earlier, on a Friday night, Rafael and I walked through central Monterrey and an area of town known as El Barrio Antiguo, famed as a hub for nightlife that once housed scores of bars, restaurants, and dance clubs. There was no one in sight. "Before," Rafael said, "these streets were filled, jam-packed on a Friday night. Now look around." Buildings were shuttered, FOR RENT signs hung on walls, entire blocks were dark and empty. A bit later, we passed a family sitting in their doorway talking. "That's another thing," Rafael said, "people used to set up chairs on the sidewalks in front of their houses to talk, drink, spend time together. It is very hot here, and at night it is often cooler outside, if you don't have air-conditioning. So people would sit outside, whole families up and down the street. But not anymore, that too is lost."

Rafael and I met on multiple occasions and spoke for hours about his experiences. When telling his story he constantly circled back to the issue of impunity, the brazen way in which the drug gang he witnessed and was then abducted by moved and operated in plain sight. "This is tangible proof of impunity and that they are the ones who call the shots in Reynosa," Rafael told me. "They can drive around in convoys, with men with assault rifles hovering in the windows, and no one says a thing. Even the way they drive is a form of impunity. They go balls-out and people clear out of the way. No one confronts them; no one gets in their way."

"In a goddamned public square they were beating us," he said at another point. "They were interrogating us, they were reloading their guns in the middle of the street. And no one even walked outside. No one looked over. Not a single police car drove by. No police or soldiers went by on patrol. The city belongs to them. And the government's discourse is 'We're going to send more troops to the border, send more soldiers.' But there is a military base right there in Reynosa! It is impossible to prove anything, but things happen that make you think there is something here that doesn't quite fit."

FOUR

Terror is the given of the place.
—Joan Didion

EL DIARIO DE JUÁREZ IS A NEWSPAPER IN MOURNING. Two newsroom desks now serve as altars honoring two murdered reporters. No one sits in these desks now. Every morning *El Diario*'s readers find printed on the newspaper's front page, just to the right of the masthead, a black ribbon tied in a bow. The text under the ribbon reads, "President Calderón: We Demand Justice for Armando and Luis Carlos." Two large printed banners hang from the roof over the front of the building facing traffic on the busy Paseo Triunfo de la República. The first carries the image of Armando "El Choco" Rodríguez and says: WE DEMAND JUSTICE FOR ARMANDO. THERE IS NO DEMOCRACY WITHOUT JOURNALISTS. The second bears the image of Luis Carlos Santiago holding a camera in the moment of taking a photograph. It reads: WHOM CAN WE ASK FOR JUSTICE? LUIS CARLOS SANTIAGO 1989–2010.

El Diario's editors first posed this question to the nation the day after a death squad killed Luis Carlos Santiago, a *Diario* photographer, and wounded a friend of his who was a photography intern at the newspaper. It was September 16, 2010, the bicentennial celebration of Mexico's independence. The two young men were finishing up their lunch break and heading back down the street to the office at 2:35 in the afternoon when the death squad gunned Luis Carlos down in the Rio Grande Mall parking lot. The gunmen fled the scene, driving down one of the main avenues of a city occupied by thousands of federal police and army troops. No one pursued Luis's killers.

The two-year anniversary of Armando Rodríguez's murder was approaching. Rodríguez was shot dead one morning in November 2008 while warming up his car; his 8-year-old daughter was in the passenger seat and witnessed his murder. No one has been arrested or put on trial. After Luis Santiago's killing and two years of waiting for justice in Armando Rodríguez's case, *El Diario* published an editorial with the headline, "Whom can we ask for justice?" Throughout the long September day that followed no one ventured an answer.

Such answers are nearly impossible to find. The Chihuahua State Attorney General's office has brought to trial less than 3 percent of the 7,341 homicide cases registered between 2008 and 2010. Most of the people detained in army and federal police operations were later released. A federal prosecutor actually posted bail for the prime suspects in the Villas de Salvárcar massacre, a case in which

gunmen slaughtered fifteen people, most of them young students, and seriously wounded another ten at a house party
in January 2010. The prosecutor was later found dead. You
can imagine, in such a climate, why *El Diario*'s editors would
not simply ask for justice, but ask to whom they could direct
their demand.

"The government is impervious to these calls for justice.
They don't hear them. They don't react to such things," said
Pedro Torres Estrada, *El Diario*'s main news editor. After
Luis Santiago's murder, he said, "We thought, okay, how can
we make them react?"

The following Sunday, September 19, *El Diario* published a front-page editorial with the following headline,
"What do you want from us?" The question was not addressed to the array of federal, state, and local officials os-
tensibly tasked with ensuring safety in the streets of Juárez,
but to the members and directors of the death squads and
assassination crews—whoever they may be—that have made
Ciudad Juárez the most murderous city in the world for two
years running.

"Señores of the different organizations disputing the
plaza of Ciudad Juárez," the front-page editorial begins
in a sober, gentlemanly tone, "the newspaper's loss of two
reporters in less than two years represents an irreparable
damage to everyone who works here and especially to the
victims' families. We would like to bring to your attention
that we are reporters, not fortune-tellers. Thus, as information workers we would like you to explain what it is that

you want from us, what you would prefer that we publish or refrain from publishing, so that we know what to bear in mind. You are, at present, the de facto authorities in this city, due to the fact that the legally established rulers have not been able to do anything to keep our colleagues from falling, despite our repeated demands that they do so. And it is for this reason that, faced with this unquestionable reality, we address you to pose this question, because what we least want is for another of our colleagues to fall victim to your bullets."

After this opening appeal to the "de facto authorities," the editorial proceeds for nearly four pages to state that the message is "not a surrender" but a truce of sorts, an attempt to understand what the rules are, for, the editors note, "even in war there are rules." The editors eviscerate the federal and state governments for their blind military strategy and failure to respond to civilian cries for justice: "The State as the protector of citizens' rights—and thus journalists' rights as well—has been absent in these bellicose years, even when it has tried to appear present through diverse [military and police] operations that in practice have been sovereign failures." The editors note that small business owners and doctors have been discussing potential tax resistance and labor strikes as drastic ways of trying to force the government to heed calls for justice, while, in contrast, "those with the highest obligation to protect citizens get lost in sterile disquisitions on whether Mexico is equal to or worse than Colombia twenty years ago, an affirmation that came from the U.S. Secretary of State Hillary Clinton and was taken up by such serious media as the *Washington Post*." The editors reserve extra venom at the end for one state politician. "And if the atrocities, assassination attempts, and intimidations against the media were not enough, yesterday the State Secretary of Education and Culture, Guadalupe Chacón Monárrez, came to rub more salt in the wound by declaring that we are responsible for the psychological terrorism with which people live here in the city."

The following day, Monday, September 20, much of the world media turned to Pedro Torres. They called from Japan. They called from London and from Amsterdam. They called from Israel, from Chile. They called from all across Colombia, the United States, and, of course, Mexico. His three cell phones and two office lines all rang at the same time, nonstop. Colleagues at the paper received calls for him on their cell phones and came knocking on his door, phones in hand.

"It was horrible, horrible, I mean . . . you can't imagine," Pedro Torres told me. "That day was frightening, profoundly. They started calling me at three in the morning that Monday and kept calling up until midnight; after twelve I didn't answer anything."

But from those whom the editors had been addressing Torres did not take a single call. The "Señores" who dispute the *plaza* never sent word. The federal government attacked the editorial in a series of press releases and press conferences in Mexico City, but not one federal official called.

"Those whom we had hoped would respond in a more positive way never did. We were really, at the end of the day, looking for a response from the government. But instead they came out very defensive," Torres said. "That was when they said that Luis Carlos's murder was not related to his profession but to some personal affair. We don't know their basis for that statement. The reality is this: Do we feel like there was an investigation? No. There wasn't. The same as in Armando's case."

While the world media turned, for a moment, to *El Diario* to ask its directors why they had written the editorial and what they hoped to achieve, federal officials only mentioned the editorial to denounce it before the international media.

"It made us angry," he said. "They don't react to reality, to events. They react to pressure in the media. This is very serious. I mean, if gunmen kill a thousand people here in a month, it won't cause any reaction from the government. But if the *New York Times* or *El País* in Spain publishes a story about it then they shout, 'Ah!' For the government this is when something happens, not when it *happens*, but when it gets published. This is a gravely serious problem."

Torres said that in the past three years of a supposed war against drug trafficking, the state and federal governments have spent "all their efforts against a perception, not against a reality. They want to win over the media with campaigns in the media. So they take action against what gets published, not what happens. This is the main problem. The government's interest is political, to win or lose sympathies amongst voters. This is a serious part of what is sustaining this mess."

Julio César Aguilar holds the record among the *nota roja* photographers in Ciudad Juárez; in one eight-hour workday he took photographs of seventeen bodies, an average of two corpses per hour in a city of 1.5 million souls. The first night that I went out riding with him in late October 2010, eight people had been executed when he started his shift at 4:00 p.m. When he picked me up after seven o'clock, he had already photographed two more. In two and a half hours we went to three more, thirteen total, an average day. After he dropped me off and finished his shift, in the predawn hours, gunmen opened fire on a bus taking maquiladora workers home after their shift, killing four and wounding fifteen, an early start on the next grim day of murder. (October 2010 would become Ciudad Juárez's most violent month on record up to that point, with 352 executions, 2,660 in the city so far that year, and some 30,000 across Mexico since Felipe Calderón first sent the army into the streets in December 2006.)

Six days a week, from Tuesday to Sunday, Julio César Aguilar—a 32-year-old who wears thick horn-rimmed glasses and button-down shirts with the sleeves rolled up to reveal tattooed forearms—drives through the most homicidal city on the planet guided by tips from colleagues and anonymous callers. He doesn't scan the police radio frequencies anymore, he said. After a massacre of six federal cops all the frequencies have been jammed. When, while driving through town, he gets a call that a body has fallen, he puts on his hazards, floors it, and disregards all manner of traffic laws. Once while he was driving, I observed him answer a call on one of his cell phones: a body. The caller, however, wasn't quite sure of the best directions out to the crime scene. Julio César reached out for a second cell phone to call another colleague and consult on the best way out to that part of the city. As he carried out both conversations simultaneously, driving thirty miles an hour through unlit Juárez back roads, he guided the steering wheel with his elbows.

In the past few years of the drug war his job has evolved into a sort of urban death race. From four in the afternoon until midnight, Julio César and his colleagues in the press crisscross the city from one end to the other, responding to anonymous calls and reports from their respective media, constantly calling each other on the road to confirm and consult, zigzagging at top speed through traffic, cruising through stop signs and red lights in deserted parts of town, navigating to and within the most marginalized areas and ultimately dealing with families and police who are not always understanding about their profession. Arriving at the scene of an execution they receive news of another. En route they get word of a *narcopinta*, or narco graffiti, or a *narcomanta*. Once there, they hear of another execution. And so they twist and race through the city until their shift is up.

Julio César has been doing photojournalism for six years, working the night shift for *El Diario* for four. He studied journalism at the Autonomous University of Chihuahua, he said, because he did not want to get stuck behind a desk. "I went into journalism because I knew that I needed to study and I didn't see myself sitting in an office," he said while driving from one execution scene to another, "I wanted a profession that would liberate me from that."

Born in Hidalgo State in central Mexico, he came with his mother and six younger brothers and sisters to Ciudad Juárez in 1988 when he was ten years old. His mother began working in the maquiladoras and studying on the weekends. Now she is a nurse. Julio César, not yet a teenager, taught himself to play the guitar and would sing for tips on Juárez city buses. Now, in a way, he has returned to working in public transit, but as a driver for the eyes of a society at once terrorized by and obsessed with the symbols of this city's daily binary lot of death and impunity: the corpses wrapped in tape, hanging from bridges, mutilated, decapitated, or posed on park benches and left in the very streets where thousands of masked federal police constantly patrol in convoys of three to five vehicles, their eyes and their machine guns ever at the ready.

The first night I rode with Julio César he photographed the scenes of three executions—one of them half a block from an elementary school—and a car wreck. The second night, he crossed Juárez completely three times to photograph a *narcopinta*, the scene of a police attack in a shopping mall parking lot, and three execution scenes. The edges of the city on these two nights were desolate, but not entirely empty. A very small number of people still sat with their families on the porch of their home, played soccer in an outdoor field, or walked down the street with a handful of friends within blocks of or just around the corner from a dead body illuminated with the red and blue lights of police sirens.

At one scene we apparently arrived only minutes after the killing of a very young man. Two men and a woman were there; one man was emotionally wrecked. Julio César and two other photographers riding with him approached the off-ramp of a highway through town where the young man's body lay twisted in the middle of the asphalt, a pool of blood extending from the head. As the photographers approached, the distraught man charged at them, screaming at them not to take pictures. No one raised their camera. The federal police officers already there approached us in combat mode with their automatic rifles aimed. Julio César, accustomed to such dynamics, walked to the other side of the police truck parked in the road and took a couple of shots of the body from there. Another federal officer approached, drawing a notebook and pen from his bulletproof vest. He asked us for our names and media outlets. Julio César asked him why he would want that information. The commander then asked, "How did you get here so quickly? Who notified you?"

Julio César—having received a call from a friend who heard the gunshots while driving—asked why the commander would ask such a question, saying that the cops never ask things like that. The commander, without raising his voice and maintaining a faint smile with every word, told us that we were part of a crime scene, not that we had arrived to a crime scene, but were part of one. "This is a crime scene," he said, pointing at us.

"Sure," Julio César responded, unfazed, "what seems strange to me is that the police never ask us such questions."

"Well," the commander said, "maybe you have never come across a commander like this," and he pointed at his own chest.

Julio César laughed and said, "Maybe you are the first one who does his job," and then after a pause identified himself, "Julio Aguilar, from *El Diario*."

The commander took down the names of the other two photographers. Not eager to have my name scribbled in that notebook, I took out my cell phone, pretended to take a call, and walked off a few steps.

The distraught man and his two companions watched us with open hostility, the kind of look that in Ciudad Juárez could immediately precede a blaze of gunfire. The photographers took a few quick shots and then we left. After crossing to the far eastern side of the city to photograph a *narcopinta* left by the Carrillo Fuentes's Juárez Cartel, known locally as La Línea, against El Chapo, we crossed to the far western edge to photograph an executed man left slouched on a park bench. Nearby, kids peered out of doorways; a few small groups ventured out and walked down the middle of the streets. Julio César received another call, a body on the street. On the drive he told me about the time he arrived at the scene of a reported execution and started taking pictures of a body splayed out in the street when the man raised his hand. Julio César froze in terror, and then realized that the man had fallen to the street not in a barrage of bullets but from booze. In Ciudad Juárez, encounters with discarded bodies of the executed have become more common than the sight of passed-out drunks.

When we arrived out at the next scene—a body left in front of a house in what appeared to be a modest middle-class neighborhood—a group of women watching us approach openly chided, "You're just now getting here? This one's been dead for more than an hour." After a few minutes of taking notes on the scene, I walked back up to the women to see if I could start up a conversation, not an easy thing to do given the circumstances. As I approached one of the women again asked in a mocking tone, "Why so late?" When I responded that, unfortunately, our delay was due to the travel time from another execution on the western edge of the city, the women changed their tone and urged us to be careful. I asked if this was the first time they had seen a dead body like this on their street and they all laughed. "No," one woman said, "just half a block from here they killed one." They told me that they had heard an argument, gunshots, and then the sound of the killers walking—not running—down the block, where a car was waiting for them.

I went to the offices of *El Diario* at noon one Sunday. The parking lot in front was entirely empty; there was no one in reception, and the door was locked. A reporter came and opened the door for me, and while we walked toward the stairs through the empty desks and cubicles on the first floor, she casually pointed out the place where everyone hid the last time a gun battle broke out in front of the office.

I went to talk with one of the reporters on the local news and crime beat, a woman who does not publish her name in a byline on most of her work. In honor of another Mexican writer who refused to keep quiet, I'll call her Rosario. Ten out of *El Diario*'s fifteen reporters are women, and they work the heaviest beats: the police and crime beat, *la nota roja*, as well as local and state politics.

Parts of Mexico are encased in silence. There are news-rooms where narcos call the shots, whether by bribe or by bullet. There are cities and entire states where publishing the name of a major drug trafficker carries an extrajudicial death sentence. Ciudad Juárez is—against all odds—no such place. Being a reporter here is a high-risk calling, and none know this better than the reporters and editors at *El Diario*, but even so, they have not bowed to silence. Rosario spoke to me in whispers at ninety miles an hour and with flawless precision.

"Here we have published the names of all the narcos on both sides of the conflict," Rosario told me from the start. "I want people to know that we haven't quieted down, that there's no silence here, that this isn't Tamaulipas."

Tucked in her cubicle, huddled over her desk Rosario showed me a computer file with her hardest-hitting stories. "Not all of them have a byline," she said, "but they were all published. Look, this is an article about the Aztecas. Many of the sources aren't named, but the story of the gang is here."

Rosario used transcripts from a court case in El Paso and went to the prison in Juárez to interview the Aztecas' leader. The Aztecas are a Juárez gang with members on both sides of the border, inside and outside of jails and prisons. The Aztecas are widely believed to move drugs across the border and carry out contract killings and other tasks for the Carrillo Fuentes's Juárez Cartel. The U.S. government suspects that members of the Aztecas killed three people linked to the U.S. Consulate in Juárez and were responsible for more than one thousand homicides in Juárez in 2009.

When Rosario arrived at the interview, the leader had fourteen men standing guard around him; all of them, she emphasized, watching her. She told them, "I only come here as a reporter. I'm not going to get you all in any kind of a mess. What I would like to know is how the gang is doing after two years of war." The leader said, "The thing is that the government declared war on us and many of our members have been disappeared, and we know that the soldiers took them out. They are covering for the other gang; they are protecting them." The leader then made an unexpected suggestion, "Let the United States come in, because they'd maybe grab us and lock us up. But here no, here they're grabbing us and they're killing us. That is what is happening, it's an extermination."

Rosario scrolled to the next article, pointing to a paragraph with all the names of mid- and high-level drug traffickers in Juárez. "For example," she said, "these are openly, the ones who are . . . in control, you know?" Using government databases and press releases she sought out the various names and realized that all of them had at one time or another been stopped or arrested. "And they let them go," she said. "Why? Who knows?" She pointed to one of the names and said, "This one for example is very dangerous. *Very* dangerous." She then read from the article out loud, "Another presumed leader of the Sinaloa Cartel who was in custody and then released and is now free and committing homicides is," and here she stopped reading and exclaimed, "Ay! How could I write that? I put 'committing homicides' . . . Did I write that?" The article goes on as follows: "Mexican army soldiers detained Gabino Salas Valenciano, alias 'The Engineer,' a 32-year-old from Durango, with drugs and guns in February 2008; the following August he was freed by the court."

"We have made a serious effort to understand the structures of the drug cartels," she went on, "who they are and how they operate. And what explains a good deal of all this is state complicity. In fact, we feel more tension from the army." She told me about an unfortunate experience she had had at an army press conference. She had brought a photograph of a civilian dressed all in black, wearing a black mask and hood, participating in a military operation in the city. She asked the general giving the press conference who the civilian in black was and who else accompanied the soldiers during their operations. The general responded, "No. The army goes out alone."

"I imagined," she told me, "that the army was using paramilitaries to identify people to, . . ." she dropped from a whisper to near soundless speech on the word "execute." "The army needed people from the other side; that was my reading." And so later during an interview with various officials and other journalists she asked the question again, and the general said, in front of everyone, "You know? You are beginning to strike me as a bit suspicious."

"You son of a bitch," she thought at the time. "It made me so angry that I couldn't say anything to him right there in the moment, but afterward I walked up to him and grabbed his arm and said, 'You know what, General? I think what you just said was totally unjust, because you know that I am only asking a question and asking questions is my job." The general looked at her for a second and then said, "Hmm. You're right." Then he walked off.

"That is the logic of the military—if you're not with me then you are with them," Rosario said. "That is dangerous and it is what the federal government is doing."

She showed me another article about the imbalance in arrests: almost all arrests involve accused members of the Juárez Cartel. At first this was only a suspicion, she said. Every time she went to a press conference where the federal police announced an arrest, the detainees stood accused of belonging to La Línea. Finally she asked a federal police commander during one of the press conferences, "It seems striking that during the last few months the federal police have only presented people from La Línea. How many have

you arrested from the other group? There *are* two groups."
No answer. Another reporter from the Mexico City—based
daily *La Jornada* repeated her question. The federal com-
missioner said, "No, no, I assure you that we are combating. . . ." Rosario interrupted him: "How many? Numbers."
He said, "Tomorrow I'll give you the count."

"And he didn't give it to us," Rosario said. "So we had
to do it ourselves."

She added up all the arrests in Juárez and shared the information with reporters from National Public Radio. NPR
then conducted its own count nationally, using the Mexican
federal attorney general's press releases announcing arrests.
Both studies showed that nearly 90 percent of those arrested
were accused of belonging to the Sinaloa Cartel's rival and
enemy drug-trafficking organizations. (As we'll see, the former Chihuahua State attorney general proceeded to release
about 90 percent of those detained.)

I asked Rosario how she made sense of all the murder.
Was it really the result of a war between two Sinaloan families? Is the federal government carrying out an extermination campaign for El Chapo? Is it pure homicidal mayhem
without reason?

"It is a lot of extermination," she said. "It is also a real
war between two groups, and a lot of the murder stems from
the impunity that allows anyone to just grab a gun. Part of
the logic of this war is that people can collect on pending
debts, or whatever, I've got a gun and I don't like you."

Luz del Carmen Sosa, 41, covers *la nota roja* for *El Diario* and has worked that beat since 1992. If Rosario speaks at 90 miles per hour, Luz del Carmen does 120. I went to speak with her at the newspaper's office one day in early November 2010 and asked her what her job was like.

"A crime scene is usually the same," she said, "the body, the ballistics. But each family's pain is distinct. I can tell you that together with my photographer, we have seen a thousand different kinds of death. All of them have been painful, especially for the families. That is the hardest thing. When you arrive before the police sometimes, or the family asks you for help, or you have to run and catch a relative so they don't faint and fall to the ground—those are hard moments. First, because that is not our purpose, our purpose is to provide information. But you are there, you are at the scene, and you can't just turn your back. That is the most difficult thing: to see how the families get destroyed; to watch how a mother screams, desperate; or to see how a child cries because they killed her parents. Recently a child . . . I had to give a child a soda and hold him because he was wounded. The baby was about one-year-and-a-half old, and his body was covered in glass. He urinated. A fireman had taken him out and handed him to a woman who then handed him to me. The boy was covered in blood and then peed all over me. I had a soda and an apple and I gave the child the soda while we waited for the ambulance. These are the things that happen and you say, 'Man, how long can this go on?' This hurts, you know? Me, as a mother—I am a mother; I have two children—this has been what impacts me the most. In all this war, this is what sticks with me: not the dead victims, but the living victims who are destroyed and whose lives are thrown up in the air. But sadly, our government has not learned anything, because they have not created institutions to deal with these types of cases. Our society is ill; it is a wounded society, a scared society that is more and more distant from this pain. And this it what makes me look for other things, other angles for information."

And she has found many. She was the first reporter to cover the collapse of Juárez's forensic medical services. She was the first reporter to write about the young female sheriff of Práxedis G. Guerrero, a story that then became a huge news boom across the world with headlines like "The Bravest Woman in the World." She is the one who updates the daily death count in Juárez—the government either does not do it or does not share its figures—which she says is "the closest thing to the reality that there is." And she keeps track of violence against women. October 2010, for example, was the worst month on record for violence against women in Juárez: forty-seven women were murdered. A total of 446 women were slain in Juárez in 2010, nearly the same number as during the entire ten-year span of 1993–2003. And yet all the nongovernmental organizations that clamored for years to end feminicide in Juárez, she said, are nowhere to be found now.

"Everyone talked and everyone stated their opinion," she said. "But now we are seeing a very active women's participation in criminal groups." She mentioned the case of a

Eunice Ramírez Contreras, a 19-year-old model who moon-lighted with a gang of kidnappers. Eunice would help select and then seduce the gang's victims. While I was interviewing reporters at *El Diario* that day, one of the reporters was flipping through Eunice's Facebook page and discovered photographs of her posing with automatic rifles in a bedroom and posing with another woman in front of a federal police car. Antonio Montana, a man who identified himself on his own Facebook page as a federal police officer, commented on a photo of Eunice in a swimsuit lying by a hotel swimming pool, "How good you look, my love." *El Diario*'s front-page headline the next day read: "Kidnapper model appears in Facebook armed and with federal police."

"You see how these young girls are getting lost in the narco-culture and you ask yourself, 'Where in hell is that girl's mother?!' Juárez is a city where you can very easily get lost, and I think this is relevant, the fact that women are more active in organized crime and there is no longer the same respect. Now they see the women as equals, and so as equals they torture them, decapitate them, burn them. This is a fact. And another fact is that all the nongovernmental organizations that always fought for 'not another murdered woman!' [*¡Ni una más!*], they have all stepped aside because they know that in this context there can really be consequences."

I asked her about the common assumption that anyone found executed was somehow dirty, and she told this story:

"They throw somebody out all wrapped in tape and it

is an execution, no? But then later you learn that the person had been kidnapped, that the family was negotiating the ransom, and that they killed the person even though the family had already paid two ransoms. And that's when they say, 'We were wrong.' That is, we judge without knowing the stories behind the events. Until it happens to us, that is when we want the benefit of the doubt. But we still haven't understood that even if someone was a drug trafficker they still have a right to life. As long as the person wasn't from your family, you like the *nota roja* and even want to see the blood and the decapitations. That is a fact. Until it happens to you, and that's when you say, 'But no, it wasn't like that.'"

At one point in our conversation Luz got a call on her cell—a report of a shoot-out and four dead bodies—and walks to another part of the office to take notes. I stared transfixed at the shelf in her cubicle against the wall, to the left of her desk. Broken and jagged pieces of seemingly random objects from crime scenes densely fill the space. A name-tag with dried blood on it. A stretch of yellow CAUTION tape. Red plastic pieces of a shattered taillight. Dozens of bullet casings, live ammunition, spent bullet casings, and bullet fragments. Wine corks and shotgun shells. A tiny Eiffel Tower and a plastic rose. Folded origami paper boats and small rocks. A bottle of spray paint and a tear gas canister.

Luz came back, saw me looking at all the objects on the shelf and started to describe them. She picked up the tag and said, "This is from Salvárcar," referring to the January 2010 massacre of fifteen students at the house party. The broken pieces of taillight came from the car where Luis Carlos Santiago was murdered. One of the bullet fragments was extracted from his friend who survived; before the friend went into surgery he pleaded with the doctor to save the bullet then lodged against his spine, so he could give it to Luz as a present for her collection. She picked up a rock and told me it came from the scene where army soldiers murdered a young boy. A sparkly purple elastic hair tie caught my eye, and I pointed to it. "That is from the first case of a woman decapitated," she said.

"This is part of the shoddy work that they do here," she added. "All of this should be in a laboratory, not here. If something is here it is because they left it behind."

The debris of impunity. I asked her why she collects it.

"So that you don't forget," she answered.

THERE WERE 3,111 KNOWN MURDERS in Ciudad Juárez in 2010, while across the border in El Paso, there were only five. The killings in Juárez have left more than 10,000 children orphaned. Between 2007 and 2010, unemployment in Juárez rose from near zero to 20 percent, more than 10,000 businesses permanently shut their doors, and 120,000 jobs vanished. In the past two years at least 100,000 and perhaps as many as 230,000 residents have fled across the border, leaving their houses and apartments abandoned.

And yet there is one sector of the Juárez economy that is humming along just great. Juárez's sweatshops, or maquiladora plants—where Mexican workers earn $5 a day on factory floors assembling imported components into for-export products—are expanding, hiring, and drawing foreign investment, undaunted by the bloodshed. Bill Conroy reported on the *Narconews* website in August 2010 that in the previous three years of murder only one homicide had taken place in the city's maquila industrial zones. Conroy called this the maquiladora exception: "There is often an exception to most rules, and in the case of Juárez, the rule of violence does not extend to its industrial zones, which are home to some 360 maquiladora factories that employ more than 190,000 people."

Tecma is an El Paso—based company that advertises "sheltering services" for foreign companies looking to out-source to Mexico. As the violence exploded in Juárez, Tecma signed new clients and made some $45 million in profit in 2009. Toby Spoon, the executive vice president of Tecma, told a reporter from the *New York Times* in December 2010 that "Juárez is open for business." Spoon lives in El Paso. He shares his schedule with no one and takes different routes each time he visits factories in Juárez. He told the *Times*, "I have discovered maybe an unsavory part of human nature: If we can make money, and it's not just too bad, then we are going to go for it."

Two things to note in Mr. Spoon's statement: first, his hubris in elevating to the status of "human nature" his discovery of something "unsavory" about his own business practices, and second, that 7,341 executions over the course of three years in a single city and the forced exodus of more than 100,000 people from their homes is "not just too bad" for him and his colleagues to keep making money. Tecma has been in business for 25 years. Apparently the more than ten years of ritual rape and murder of female maquiladora workers in Juárez that preceded the current homicide epidemic was also "not just too bad."

It should not surprise that the Juárez-based maquiladora industry would surge unaffected by the murder and chaos all around it. Maquiladoras and illegal drug trafficking are two gears in one economy, and in Juárez those gears meet and turn together. More than 2,000 trucks and 34,000 cars cross from Juárez into El Paso every day. In 2009, more than $42 billion in legal trade crossed between Juárez and El Paso. An estimated $1.5 million to $10 million worth of illegal drugs moves over the border from Juárez to El Paso *every single day*. How do you think the drugs—bulky, heavy packages of cocaine, marijuana, heroin, and crystal meth—get across? Where does the infrastructure and organizational capacity exist to transport so much merchandise? On the backs of mules led out through the desert? In the backpacks of pedestrians? In the trunks or spare tires of SUVs and sedans going through customs? Sure, there are the occasional sensational discoveries of underground tunnels. But what about the thousands of daily cargo trucks with their NAFTA fast passes? What about the maquiladora warehouses? Recall, when *Forbes* first listed El Chapo Guzmán on its list of billionaires, the magazine, with no moral qualms or qualifiers, credited the source of his fortune as "shipping."

Writer Charles Bowden called this place "the laboratory of our future" back in 1998 when he and a group of Juárez photographers published a book by that name chronicling the city's impoverished sweatshop workforce, migrants, drug-related executions, and feminicide in the wake of NAFTA. "The book was strongly criticized by the government at the time," said Julián Cardona, one of the Juárez-based photographers who worked on the book. "But now the present is so much worse than what was shown and described in the book. In other words, we were right, but few paid attention."

Julián Cardona has worked as a photographer in Juárez since 1993. He shot for *El Diario* from 1993 to 2000. He has published several photography books with texts by Charles Bowden and has contributed photos for Bowden's magazine articles and his recent book about Ciudad Juárez, *Murder City*.

In March 2008, Julián Cardona set out to document every homicide that took place that month. There were 181. Of those, he said, seventy-seven were corner boys, small-time local dealers. "El Chapo ordering the murder of corner boys?" he asked, incredulous. This would be like Bill Gates ordering the firing of computer salespeople at Best Buys in Los Angeles. "It's absurd," he told me. "These were poor people, corner boys. Many were tortured. There were executions before, but this was something unprecedented."

Julián urged that one take a broader view than the gang war and cops-and-robbers explanation given by the government and repeated uncritically in the U.S. press. "It is important to emphasize the local factors that are kept out of public scrutiny: land speculation, the local oligarchy, and four decades of political manipulation of a global economic scheme. This has been an equation: land profits plus exploitation of cheap labor equals criminal machine. We can't evade the fact that the city chose to be a maquila. And when I say the city I don't mean the citizens, I mean the elite. If the problem could really be reduced to Chapo versus Vicente or good versus bad then the rest of society and the economy would be fine. What the citizens of Juárez are suffering is much worse than that. This is the manifestation of a failed state incapable of providing security, justice, or peace, where the role of the state has been taken on by a kind of parallel state where extortion and kidnapping are used instead of taxes. This is happening in other regions of Mexico. In Juárez, the state cannot guarantee the security of its citizens; it has lost the monopoly on violence."

In late October 2010 when I arrived in Juárez, the top story in the news was a series of YouTube videos of former Chihuahua state Attorney General Patricia González Rodríguez's brother, Mario Ángel, calming answering the questions of an off-camera voice while sitting handcuffed and surrounded by five masked men in desert fatigues aiming assault rifles at his head and body. Mario Ángel appeared unharmed in the video and spoke with a strangely matter-of-fact tone of voice and always with precise information. Among the many revelatory declarations in the first video was Mario Ángel's testimony regarding the former governor, José Reyes Baeza, and his own sister, Patricia González Rodríguez, indicating their direct involvement with the Juárez Cartel, use of their offices to protect the cartel's personnel, shipments, and, in Patricia's case, direct involvement in the assassination of Armando Rodríguez. State prosecutors under Patricia González's command released more than 9,500 suspects of the 10,000 detained or arrested during the federal Chihuahua Joint Operation. Mario Ángel's body was later found in a shallow grave on the outskirts of town. (The video can hardly be taken as courtroom evidence, nor Mario Ángel's statements as having been made freely and in the general interest of truth. That said, such narco videos have a disturbing record of disclosing accurate information, and it would be a mistake to simply disregard the accusations.)

With all this violence, impunity, and intrigue, one might half expect to see roving death squads firing on pedestrians and writhing bodies on sidewalks while riding from the airport into town. But the only constant sign to the outsider's eye that something is terribly wrong here is the heavy, militarized police presence—federal police convoys of large pickup trucks carrying masked, battle-ready officers with machine guns poised in the back. Seeing these convoys every time you step outside, seeing them anywhere and everywhere you go at any time of day or night, leads to a haunting question: how can so many people get shot down, so many bodies get dumped, and yet so few people get caught in the act with all these cops roaming about?

One of the most striking features of Ciudad Juárez is that in the grip of so much terror it is still a "functioning" city. People still go to work and to school. City buses still make their routes. While I was there you could still take a walk in the morning to pick up the paper and sit outside with a cup of coffee and not have to duck bullets. But you couldn't take that walk without thinking that getting shot was an actual, and not all that remote, possibility. It is a battered and terrified city, but it has not yet surrendered.

Quite the opposite: there are more mobilizations against Calderón's drug war in Ciudad Juárez than anywhere else. And the stakes for participating in such mobilizations are much higher there. A few days after I arrived, a small march of about two hundred people was nearing the campus of the Autonomous University of Ciudad Juárez. The march was part of the opening ceremonies of a three-day conference called "The International Forum vs. Militarization and Violence," organized by a coalition of student, doctor, teacher, and progressive organizations. A small group of young students ran up ahead of the march to spray-paint images on the walls of a PRI office building across the street from campus. Almost immediately a federal police convoy sped around the corner and sent the students running across the street to campus. Several officers jumped out of the back of the truck and pursued the students. In Mexico, with its history of student massacres, it is against the law for police to enter an autonomous university campus—universities hire their own security. The federal police followed the students through the university entrance gate and then almost immediately opened fire on them from behind. Nineteen-year-old sociology student José Darío Álvarez took a bullet in the back and collapsed on the asphalt of the campus drive. The bullet, a 7.62 high-caliber bullet fired at close range from the police-issue G-3 assault rifle, opened a hole in José Darío's stomach the size of his hand. Still conscious, he tried to gather up and hold his intestines in place. The police officer stood over his body, apparently stunned for a second, and then attempted to lift him up. Another officer approached to help him; both were masked.

Pavel Vásquez, a 23-year-old elementary school teacher, and Violeta Cangas, a 27-year-old general physician, were in Violeta's car at the university gate entrance when the students and police sprinted past them. They heard the shot and flinched with fright. When Pavel looked up he saw José Darío fall to the ground. At first he thought that the police had fired tear gas or rubber bullets, but when he got out of the car and ran up to José Darío he realized the mistake.

"When I came up to see him," Pavel told me, "I saw that his intestines were hanging out. The police officer approached and, you know if [the police] shot him then I doubt he's there to help him. My friend got out of the car and pushed the cop aside shouting, 'Look what you did, asshole! Everyone film him; take his picture!'"

As more students and witnesses gathered, they prevented the federal police from taking José Darío away and started making frantic calls for an ambulance. Several students, understandably enraged, shouted insults and threw rocks at the police vehicles still parked across the street. The police aimed their guns at the students and fired several shots in the air. The students shouted, "You're here to kill us, not defend us!" Press photographers arriving with the march took photos of this moment, which led to a briefly held mistaken view that the police had opened fire on the students *after* the latter had confronted them. The ambulance dispatcher kept hanging up on the callers, and after about fifteen minutes Violeta, Pavel, and a professor from the medical school lifted José Darío into Violeta's car and sped him off to the hospital, saving his life. (Over the course of several days, he survived multiple reconstructive surgeries.)

The federal police first tried to obfuscate the events by putting out a press release combining two different events that took place in distant parts of the city and at distinct times. They seemed at pains to somehow link shooting a 19-year-old student protester in the back to the drug war. Pedro Torres of *El Diario* brought this to my attention—I hadn't seen the first press release—and said, "I thought that the federal police were putting too much emphasis on the fact that they came from a different part of the city. To me, that says that actually they were following the march. They say more with what they don't say that with what they say." Next the federal police said that the officers saw a group of "masked men" and fired shots in the air. José Darío was not masked, though the police officer who shot him was.

I spoke with Pavel and Violeta the following morning

at the scene of the crime. As they walked me through the events they pointed to the bullet casings still on the pavement and the pool of blood where José Darío fell, a few yards inside the university grounds. No one had conducted a crime-scene investigation. The municipal police arrived three hours after the fact and then left without gathering any evidence. Students made a wide ring of bricks and rocks around the pool of blood. One of the pieces of brick held down a hand-scrawled sign that read: EVIDENCE.

"Spray-painting a wall is no reason to shoot somebody," Pavel said, standing over the bloodstain. "We live in a fucking city where every day *at least* three people are executed, where convoys of armed commandos with up to five vehicles will drive away from the crime scene, and yet a city where not more than five minutes go by without a damn federal police convoy driving by, and they don't arrest anybody. There are police roadblocks throughout the city. Military searches. Disappearances. But never, never do they arrest and convict somebody. They tell us that this is a war against drug trafficking. A war is a confrontation between two enemies. There is no confrontation here. Here there are paramilitary groups killing people. And how strange that the ones they kill are poor and young. And the government doesn't give us any explanation beyond 'The dead were up to something.' And with that the government links you to organized crime. But we know that is not the case, and even if it were, it is no justification for execution. Come on! There is the rule of law, so detain them, put them on trial, sentence them. But don't send paramilitaries out to kill them. . . . There is no war on drugs. In Juárez, there are paramilitary groups shooting us dead, compañero."

The student organizations planning the antimilitarization forum called for another protest march for the evening of November 2, 2010, Day of the Dead. More than two thousand people heeded the call. Some people on the left are tired of marches. I once read a hostile comment on a website where I had posted photographs of a massive march in Oaxaca. "Another cattle drive," it said. In places like Mexico City barely a week goes by without a march of a few thousand people grinding traffic to a halt. But in Ciudad Juárez—with its daily executions and only three days after police shot a student protester in the back—marching through the streets at night handing out flyers and shouting chants against the federal government's murderous militarized drug policy is risky political action. The march was aimed at the protesters' fellow city dwellers as much as at the federal government, and the message was a call to overcome fear and take back the city. People driving by in their cars, waiting for buses, walking down the sidewalks, either honked their horns or cheered the students on. The federal police kept mostly out of sight.

Many of the protesters wore elaborate handmade Day of the Dead costumes. One young woman, dressed as a melancholy grim reaper, held a sign that read: ENOUGH! LET ME REST.

FIVE

At the forefront of our minds, the obvious signals of violence are acts of crime and terror, civil unrest, international conflict. But we should learn to step back to disentangle ourselves from the fascinating lure of this directly visible 'subjective' violence, violence performed by a clearly identifiable agent. We need to perceive the contours of the background which generates such outbursts. A step back enables us to identify a violence that sustains our very efforts to fight violence and promote tolerance.

—Slavoj Žižek

In Mexico today tuberculosis kills more people than AK-47s, but the sound of the daily bloodshed wrought by this illness of poverty remains silent.

—Diego Osorno

G.W.F. HEGEL SAID THAT THE MONUMENTAL EVENTS in world history occur twice. Karl Marx later commented that Hegel forgot to add that the first time they occur as tragedy, the second time as farce. Reagan's drug war was an overwhelming tragedy; Calderón's is a farce. The tragedy of mass incarceration, community degradation, and decades of brutality and murder at the hands of U.S.-supported

counterinsurgencies and military dictatorships throughout the hemisphere is now being repeated as the farce of
senseless murder, a so-called "narco-insurgency" south of
the border. Techniques and expertise acquired from decades
of U.S. military training and assistance, meant to aid Latin
American armies and death squads in their elimination of
leftists and anyone labeled communist, have been diverted
and perverted to serve the illegal drug industry: ritual beheadings; massacres of children, families, bystanders, and
migrants; the brutal use of torture. Slavoj Žižek, in his book
First as Tragedy, Then as Farce, reminds us that Herbert
Marcuse "added yet another turn of the screw" to Hegel's
comment, "Sometimes, the repetition in the guise of a farce
can be more terrifying than the original tragedy."

A terrifying farce. What better way to understand
the Zetas? About thirty men, originally trained by U.S.
and Israeli commandos to be elite Mexican special forces
counterinsurgency operatives after the 1994 Zapatista upris-
ing in Chiapas, abandoned ranks, went to work for the Gulf
Cartel, recruited heavily from the Mexican military and
Guatemalan counterinsurgency forces known as Kaibiles,
completely altered the practices of cartel violence with their
brutal and spectacular torture and execution techniques, and
then staged a coup against the Gulf Cartel and went on a
murder spree that included the indiscriminate slaughter of
seventy-two Central and South American migrants in a barn
in Tamaulipas. A terrifying farce. What better way to understand the Mexican Army's participation in the drug war? The

same institution that created the Sinaloa drug capos—by bowing to U.S. pressure to carry out defoliation campaigns, but then raiding, raping, and pillaging villages throughout the Sierra Madre in the 1970s—thirty years later, during Calderón's drug war, is doing the capos' dirty work. The army went to Ciudad Juárez soon after the Sinaloa Cartel had arrived to conquer that *plaza*, and many Mexican reporters and analysts I spoke to said that the army's deployment was intended to back up El Chapo against his rivals. But here is the salient fact: after some ten thousand soldiers of the Mexican Army arrived in Juárez, the execution rate nearly *doubled*. The army mostly withdrew; in its stead five thousand federal police occupied the city, and the execution rate continued its grim rise.

And then there is Obama. Reagan was a tragedy: his drug war unleashed forces that have wrecked millions of lives throughout the entire hemisphere. But what will Barack Obama become? He arrived with "hope" and "change" and then largely pursued the same prohibition, "supply control," and "law enforcement" policies that have reigned since Reagan, though with a few notable differences—he stepped away from the bellicose rhetoric of drug wars, indicated that his administration would not target medical marijuana practices in those states where they are legal, and signed the 2010 Fair Sentencing Act—that do not challenge the dominance of the drug war ideology. For at the same time his administration stopped using the term "drug war," it stepped up military aid ($830 million in 2009) to Mexico's army and federal police for the now unspoken drug war and further militarized the border. Perhaps the pinnacle of farce is Secretary of State Hillary Clinton's proclaimed concern about a budding "narco-insurgency" in Mexico. . . .

But let's step back.

Mexico's economy is in shambles. More than 51 percent of the population lives in poverty. Ten million people fell below the poverty line between 2006 and 2009, according to a 2009 World Bank report. In the second trimester of 2009 the Mexican economy shrank by 10.3 percent, a fall not seen in seventy-five years. In 2008 alone 12,850 businesses closed and 8,310 people died of malnutrition, that is, hunger. Between 2000 and July 2009, the number of manufacturing jobs in Mexico declined by 27 percent, a loss of some 1.1 million jobs. Meanwhile, one in three Mexican workers labors in the so-called informal economy—where defiance and bribes replace permits and taxes—which grew by nearly a million jobs from 2008 to 2009. And yet the maquiladoras in Juárez are "open for business," Mexican telecommunications tycoon Carlos Slim remains the world's richest man, and the U.S. Drug Enforcement Agency estimates that between $18 billion and $39 billion of illicit *cash* is smuggled across the border into Mexico every year, with $10 billion to $25 billion successfully laundered into the Mexican financial system annually.

The United States and Mexican governments continue spending billions of dollars on police and military campaigns that have no rival in history in terms of their absolute failure. More people use drugs than ever before. At the time of this writing, fifteen states in the United States have some form of legalized marijuana for medicinal use. In October 2010, California reduced marijuana possession from a misdemeanor to a civil infraction. In 2009, Mexico decriminalized minor possession of marijuana, cocaine, heroin, methamphetamines, and LSD.

Calderón took office in December 2006, exactly six years after the end of seventy-one years of one-party rule. Mexico was supposed to be a full-fledged democracy. That year, however, was one of mass protest mobilizations and extreme acts of state violence. State police arrested and raped more than twenty women taken prisoner in San Salvador Atenco on May 4, 2006. Oaxaca state police death squads killed at least seventeen people during a five-month teachers' strike that controlled Oaxaca City until federal police were sent in to repress the movement. The presidential election itself was the cause of massive protests alleging fraud and calling for a full, vote-by-vote recount. Calderón's less-than-one-percentage-point victory was challenged in court and in the streets. The federal electoral court ordered a recount in only 9 percent of precincts and later declared Calderón the winner. Calderón had to sneak into the Mexican Senate at midnight, take his oath, and flee through a back door to avoid protesters. During his first days in office he raised the salaries of the military's top brass, appeared in military uniform at a parade, and sent the army into the streets to wage a war on the drug business.

Just over three years later, in March 2010, Calderón told CNN, "My main objective is not to do away with drugs or eliminate their consumption. That is impossible. My objective is to strengthen Mexican law. I want to make Mexico a country where the law is respected, because that is the first step to development." To "strengthen Mexican law" Calderón sent the army and federal police into the streets to unleash a war that, by May 2011, had left more than 38,000 people dead, 38,000 families shattered, and some 50,000 children orphaned, with an impunity rate for all these murders of at least 95 percent and an accompanying drastic increase in all manner of crime from kidnapping to oil theft.

All talk of law and order in the drug war battlefields where 16-year-old kids roam the streets with AR-15 assault rifles following orders like, "Kill every last fucking one of them," where one of the principal combat tactics in the trafficking zones is to "heat up" enemy territory by massacring innocent people, where five thousand federal police constantly patrol the city with the highest homicide rate in the world—and that rate keeps going up—where 95 percent of the murders are not even being investigated, all such talk of strengthening the law is simply bullshit.

Calderón sent the army into the streets to protect him, seeking to grasp through the exercise of violence the social legitimacy he never achieved through the ballot box. The army meanwhile does what it has always done with drug traffickers; sell the plaza to one group and eliminate that group's rivals.

And in the United States, what is all this talk of prohibition as the only way to address health concerns, crime rates, and keeping children safe where decades of narcotics prohibition has produced the highest number of drug users in history, the largest prison population in the world—disproportionately people of color—and police forces that subsidize themselves from assets seized during drug-busts? In these battlefields, all discourse about prohibition as a public safety policy is self-serving, fundamentalist lies tantamount to complicity in the intellectual authorship of perpetual mass murder.

Let us be clear, absolute prohibition is legislated death.

So what do we know? After decades of a multinational drug war imposed by the United States government, illegal plants, fungi, and chemicals are more plentiful and more people consume them than ever before. Profits generated by this illegal market pulse through the legal capitalist economy and keep it afloat when speculative markets crash. The United States has the largest prison population in the world. And Mexico—the gateway to the United States drug market—is being bludgeoned with murder.

U.S. policy has not stopped the flow of drugs, but it has outsourced most of the killing. Judging by the drug war's own proclaimed objectives, there is no better case study in failure. But it is not a failure, of course; illegality increases the value of the commodity, and illegality allows for massive funding of police and military repression and mechanisms of social control. The drug war is a horrid success of state violence and capitalist accumulation, a cash-intoxicated marketplace that simply budgets for murder and political graft to keep things running smoothly.

And if the myths and rhetoric of good guys and bad, cops and robbers, are so completely inadequate for gaining any understanding of the scale and nature of the misery, murder, and destruction of the drug war, what reorientation could lead to understanding and thus possible solutions? What questions could prove helpful? What if the persistent and colossal failure of the drug war reveals less about the lengths people will go to get high, the relationship between people and psychoactive alkaloids, effective law-enforcement strategies, or criminal behavior than it does about endemic problems in the structures of our basic economic and political systems? What if illegal drug businesses are not a threat to the state and capitalism, but a covert and powerful lifeline? If people agree on finding a way to end the abhorrent brutality of the drug war, then doesn't the fact that states and capital markets benefit so tremendously from that war warrant serious analysis?

And so we come to the various proposals for decriminalization, legalization, and regulation. The end of prohibition, however, does not signal the disappearance of very real problems associated with substance abuse and chemical addiction. Legalization will address the problems *created by prohibition*: rampant murder, regions of absolute impunity, mass incarceration, disguised repression, and a pretext for U.S. interference in drug-producing countries, among others. Opponents of legalization will list the social and individual problems associated with drug abuse as reasons for prohibition. We now know that such an argument is ridiculous. Prohibition enjoys a track record of failure spanning more than a century, during which time it has set in motion a host of devastating problems far worse than the ones its advocates claim to solve. Unfortunately, prohibition and the drug war propagated to enforce it are good politics for Democrats and Republicans who want to appear "tough on crime," even though prohibition propels far more crime than the mere use of marijuana, cocaine, or heroin.

Legalization is not a fringe proposal. The *Economist* magazine, Yale law professor Steven B. Duke writing in the *Wall Street Journal*, former Mexican presidents Ernesto Zedillo and Vicente Fox, and the centrist Mexican magazine *Nexos* have all advocated for various legalization proposals. Legalization will solve one set of problems, but it will leave two other spheres untouched. First, individuals and communities will continue to suffer from substance abuse, as they do now with problems related to consuming legal drugs like alcohol and tobacco. However, with prohibition and the drug war over, real issues of substance abuse could be addressed through education, harm reduction, and public health measures without having to hide, scrounge for funding, or risk jail time for giving someone a clean syringe.

Legalization will do nothing, however, to address the second problem, the underlying economic and social violence that has motivated U.S. prohibition efforts and drug wars throughout the twentieth century. Bringing pot and cocaine into the legal market economy's open arms will stop the gangland murders but leave Mexico, for example, to the good old days of living under a bloody authoritarian regime that bows to U.S. economic bullying, concentrates wealth in a tiny fraction of the population while sinking the majority in destitution and misery, prompts the mass exodus of nearly half a million jobless souls annually, and brutally crushes organized resistance. One can imagine a new wave of child laborers fleeing economic destitution and political violence in Guerrero to pick marijuana buds in Sinaloa (where they already pick tomatoes) for a company owned by the world's richest man, Carlos Slim (who already controls Mexico's tobacco industry) and sold abroad in slick $20 packs of rolled joints.

And this is what should be fought: a future of hunger, forced migration, and thinly disguised slave labor. Not the drug war. For the drug war—as designed, waged, and imposed on other nations by the U.S. government—is not a war of political beliefs, of manifestos and declarations, a war for homeland, defense of nation, or liberation. The drug war is a proxy war for racism, militarization, social control, and access to the truckloads of cash that illegality makes possible. The drug war itself is a violent criminal enterprise. To stand by and watch it rage is to step inside the silence that hangs over every anonymous death, bow our heads, and wait our turn.

IT WOULD TAKE A NAME. Police got the call at 6:20 a.m. on March 28, 2011. They dove out to the scene and pulled seven dead bodies from a Honda sedan on Brisas de Tampico Street near the Cuernavaca-Mexico City highway. Bodies were stuffed in the front and back seats. Bodies were stuffed in the trunk. Their hands and feet were bound. Asphyxiated, the autopsies would conclude. The police reported finding a poster board sign in the car threatening the Mexican military and signed "CDG." (Later that night banners signed CDG would appear in Cuernavaca denying responsibility for the killings.) The police did not release the exact words written on the poster board. But the intended message—whoever its authors were—was clear: death. Nameless death.

But the names were waiting there in that car. And one name would break the siege of custom and silence, Juan Francisco Sicilia Ortega.

Juan Francisco's father is Javier Sicilia, a well-known and respected novelist, journalist, and poet. Juan Francisco, age 24, was not another nameless dead youth. He was, in the eyes of Mexico's mass media, the son of a poet. The first news reports informed that seven bodies were found dead, but gave only one name. Mexico City's *El Universal* wrote on March 29, 2011, "The Morelos state Attorney General confirmed that Juan Francisco Sicilia Orteda, 24 years-old, son of the journalist and writer Javier Sicilia, was among the victims." The names of these six victims were left out: Julio César Romero Jaimes, Luis Antonio Romero Jaimes,

Álvaro Jaimes Avelar, Jaime Gabriel Alejo Cadena, María del Socorro Estrada Hernández, and Jesús Chávez Vázquez.

The Morelos state authorities first announced that the killings appeared to have been a "settling of accounts" between drug traffickers. They soon rushed to clarify that Jose Francisco was not involved in any illicit activity. Two days after the killings the local Cartel del Pacifico Sur, or CPS, hung banners in town denying responsibility. One local blog (http://notaroja-koneocho.blogspot.com) posted that two of the young men killed, Gabriel Alejo and Luis Antonio Romero Jaimes, had been beaten and robbed by armed men who identified themselves as state police officers and threatened to kill the young men if they reported the crime. One local police officer commented that the victims appeared to have been asphyxiated slowly, using tourniquets, a method, he said, unseen before in executions in Cuernavaca. Rumors flew that the Army was involved. But the official reaction was again that of the presumed guilt of the dead; "it was a settling of accounts."

In a classist political culture the poor mothers and fathers of the dead are almost as nameless as their murdered children. Rarely will the microphones and cameras seek them out. And rarely will they wish to speak in a place where the killers act with absolute impunity. The poet was different. The microphones and cameras sought and found him. And he spoke out.

On March 28, 2011 Javier Sicilia was attending a poetry conference in Manila when he heard that his son had been murdered. On his long trip to Manila he had a four-teen-hour layover in Amsterdam. He walked through the red light district and saw people buying and selling drugs. He did not see anyone firing AK-47s. He did not see any dead bodies being pulled from the trunks of cars. He would describe this vision to President Felipe Calderón, who asked to see him upon his return. He would tell Calderón that in Amsterdam people buy and sell drugs and they do not kill each other; what Calderón has done with his drug war is shameful and has no pardon. Calderón would respond, in so many words, you are right; I was mistaken, but there is no turning back now.

Javier Sicilia would not turn back. In that rare media opening that gave him the opportunity to speak to millions, he said his son's name and the names of his son's friends, and in so doing reminded a wounded nation that behind the swelling statistic human beings with names and loved ones lie dead. And then he decried the murder, the impunity, the idiocy of prohibition; he railed against the United States government's blind eye toward arms trafficking into Mexico and Felipe Calderón's entirely failed war. He wrote an "open letter to politicians and criminals" widely reprinted and discussed across Mexico in which he told them that he and his nation were completely fed up, exhausted, and repulsed with all the murder and impunity, that they had had enough. He called for people to take to the streets on April 6, 2011 and march against violence, march against the so-called drug war.

Tens of thousands of people in some forty Mexican cities answered his call. In Cuernavaca alone, more than 20,000 people filled the streets in one of the largest demonstrations in that city's history. One of the many signs held up during the April 6 march in Cuernavaca read, "Mexico, wake up! Indifference kills." Another read, "If they don't kill me, the fear will." Another read, "Our deceased demand our justice. Legalize drugs now!" And yet another, "Some parents are poets, but all the children are poetry. No more blood." The march paused in front of the military base in Cuernavaca, where Javier Sicilia stood on top of a truck and addressed the crowd, "Our dead are not statistics," he said, "they are not numbers. They are human beings with names."

Javier Sicilia used his position of fame and unspeakable pain to carve his son's name into a wall of indifference, to wedge his son's name into a country's misery and in so doing pry open a space for all the names of the dead to be spoken, for the indifference to fall. On April 12, 2011, on the walls of the state government palace in Cuernavaca, Sicilia drilled a metal plaque bearing his son's name into the stone. He then drilled six other plaques into the wall bearing the names of those killed with his son. He called on the people of Morelos to come and drill more names of people killed in the so-called drug war into this same wall. Within hours others had put up ninety-six plaques. He called on people across Mexico to drill similar memorials into the walls of government palaces throughout the country. He called on people everywhere in Mexico to stand up and demand an end to the murder, an end to the prohibition regime, an end to the drug war.

A rebellion of names in a war of anonymous death.

A war that rages on. In April 2011, while Javier Sicilia spoke names into the drug-war dark, forensics teams were searching out mass graves in San Fernando, Tamaulipas, the same city of 60,000 where drugland killers executed seventy-two migrants in a barn in August 2010. By the end of April 2011, the forensics workers dug out 183 bodies. Most of the dead had been traveling by bus on a toll-free highway. Armed men stopped the buses at military-style roadblocks, removed the passengers they wanted, robbed them, perhaps tried to recruit them, killed them with sledgehammer and iron-rod blows to the head, and then buried their bodies in huge mass graves. Nameless dead.

Journalist Marcela Turati traveled to the morgue in Matamoros, Tamaulipas to interview family members of missing persons standing in line to learn the identities of the recovered bodies. In an article published in *Proceso* on April 17, 2011, Turati quotes a woman bringing bottled water to the out-of-state people waiting in line who said furiously, "There have been many denunciations [of what was happening along the highway] but no one heard us, it was like speaking under water." Morgue officials asked the more than 400 family members waiting in line to prepare descriptions of their loved ones's clothing, jewelry, or tattoos. The bodies were "no longer recognizable due to the passing of time and the conditions of their deaths." One morgue official told Turati that the dead were all of the marginalized class. "They didn't have the money to pay the toll fees and take faster highways, and no one wanted to learn what was happening because they weren't the sons of anyone famous," the man said.

Murder, impunity, and the mass grave of indifference. This is precisely what Javier Sicilia and people throughout Mexico are up against. And from their grief and rage a movement is growing. The movement has roots in Ciudad Juárez where for more than two years people have taken to the streets in marches and organized community-based refuges from the violence. It has roots in the work of journalists who risk everything to report stories that pierce the silence. It has roots in women like Alma Trinidad who refuse to go home and cry. And it has roots in people like Salomón Monárrez and Meché Murillo who look death in the face and keep fighting.

A name and a poet's courage have taken on the indifference surrounding drug war murder. It will take a movement to stop it. That movement has begun.

SOURCES

Most of the material in this book comes from interviews and observations. Source information for quoted or referenced material is provided in the body of the text. I used the following Mexican media outlets to corroborate facts gathered in interviews as well as to monitor the daily and weekly news events: *El Diario de Juárez*, *El Sur de Guerrero*, *El Universal*, *La Jornada*, *Milenio*, *Proceso*, and *Riodoce*.

Alexander, Michelle. *The New Jim Crow: Mass Incarceration in the Age of Colorblindness*. New York: The New Press, 2010.

Astorga, Luis. *El siglo de las drogas: Usos, percepciones, y personalidades*. Mexico City: Espasa-Hoy, 1996.

Baum, David. *Smoke and Mirrors: The War on Drugs and the Politics of Failure:* Boston: Little Brown, 1996.

Bowden, Charles. *Juárez: The Laboratory of Our Future*. New York: Aperture, 1998.

———. *Down By the River: Drugs, Money, Murder, and Family*. New York: Simon and Schuster, 2004.

———. *Murder City: Ciudad Juárez and the Global Economy's New Killing Fields*. New York: Nation Books, 2010.

Campbell, Howard. *Drug War Zone: Frontline Dispatches from the Streets of El Paso and Juárez*. Austin: University of Texas Press, 2009.

Cockburn, Alexander and Jeffrey St. Clair. *Whiteout: The CIA, Drugs, and the Press*. New York: Verso, 1998.

Davenport-Hines, Richard. *The Pursuit of Oblivion: A Global History of Narcotics*. New York: W.W. Norton & Company, 2004.

Didion, Joan. *Salvador*. New York: Vintage International, 1994.

Hernández, Anabel. *Los señores del narco*. Mexico City: Grijalbo, 2010.

Gootenberg, Paul. *Andean Cocaine: The Making of a Global Drug*. Chapel Hill: The University of North Carolina Press, 2008.

———. "Talking Like a State: Drugs, Borders, and the Language of Control," in Van Schendel, Willem and Itty Abraham, eds. *Illicit Flows and Criminal Things: States, Borders, and the Other Side of Globalization*. Bloomington and Indianapolis: Indiana University Press, 2005.

Guillermoprieto, Alma. *Looking for History: Dispatches from Latin America*. New York: Vintage Books, 2001.

Kapuscinski, Ryszard. *Cristo con un fusil al hombro*. Barcelona: Anagrama, 2010.

Lomnitz, Claudio. *Death and the Idea of Mexico*. New York: Zone Books, 2005.

McCoy, Alfred. *The Politics of Heroin: CIA Complicity in the Global Drug Trade*. Rev. ed. Chicago: Lawrence Hill Books, 2003.

Musto, David F. *The American Disease: Origins of Narcotics Control*. Third ed. New York: Oxford University Press, 1999.

Osorno, Diego. *El cartel de Sinaloa: El uso político del narco*. Mexico City: Grijalbo, 2009.

Poppa, Terrence E. *Drug Lord: The Life and Death of a Mexican Kingpin*. El Paso: Cinco Puntos Press, 2010.

Ravelo, Ricardo. *Los capos: Las narco-rutas de México*. Mexico City: Plaza Janés, 2005.

———. *Herencia maldita: El reto de Calderón y el Nuevo mapa del narcotráfico*. México: Grijalbo, 2007.

Schou, Nick. *Kill the Messenger: How the CIA's Crack-Cocaine Controversy Destroyed Journalist Gary Webb*. New York: Nation Books, 2006.

Simon, David and Edward Burns. *The Corner: A Year in the Life of an Inner-City Neighborhood*. New York: Broadway Books, 1998.

Turati, Marcel. *Fuego Cruzado: Las víctimas atrapadas en la guerra del narco*. Mexico City: Grijalbo, 2011.

Valdez Cárdenas, Javier. *Miss Narco: Belleza, poder y violencia: Historias reales de mujeres en el narcotráfico mexicano*. Mexico City: Aguilar, 2009.

Žižek, Slavoj. *Violence: Six Sideways Reflections*. London: Profile Books, 2008.

———. *First as Tragedy, Then as Farce*. New York: Verso, 2009.

ACKNOWLEDGMENTS

For all those fighting against the reign of terror that is the drug war. Van abrazos fuertes, del corazón: Diego and El Froy; Javier, Ismael, and Alejandro; Alma and César; Meché and Salomón; Pepis, Juan Carlos, and Marco; Luis; Ray; Sergio and Lenin; Gloria and Jacobo; Julio César, Rosario, Luz, Pedro, and Rocio; Beni; Ted and Kirsten; Greg; Charles and Rita; Diana; Bear and Rux; Suzanna; Bob; Drew; Mitch; Gringoyo; Jonathan; Allaire; and Nanea.

John Gibler is a writer based in Mexico and California, the author of *Mexico Unconquered: Chronicles of Power and Revolt* (City Lights Books, 2009), and a contributor to *País de muertos: Crónicas contra la impunidad* (Random House Mondadori, 2011). He is a correspondent for KPFA in San Francisco and has published in magazines in the United States and Mexico, including *Left Turn*, *Z Magazine*, *Earth Island Journal*, *ColorLines*, *Race, Poverty, and the Environment*, *Fifth Estate*, *New Politics*, *In These Times*, *Yes! Magazine*, *Contralínea*, and *Milenio Semanal*.

Open Media is a movement-oriented publishing project committed to the vision of "one world in which many worlds fit"—a world with social justice, democracy, and human rights for all people. Founded during wartime in 1991 by Greg Ruggiero, Open Media has a history of producing critically acclaimed and best-selling titles that address the most urgent political and social issues of our time.

City Lights Open Media Series
www.citylights.com/collections/openmedia/